SPEAKING THE UNSPEAKABLE

Essays on Sexuality, Gender, and Holocaust Survivor Memory

D1606337

Jonathan C. Friedman

University Press of America,® Inc.
Lanham · New York · Oxford

Copyright © 2002 by
University Press of America,® Inc.
4501 Forbes Boulevard
Suite 200
Lanham, Maryland 20706
UPA Acquisitions Department (301) 459-3366

PO Box 317
Oxford
OX2 9RU, UK

Library of Congress Cataloging-in-Publication Data

Friedman, Jonathan C., 1966-
Speaking the unspeakable : essays on sexuality, gender, and Holocaust
Survivor memory / Jonathan C. Friedman.
p.   cm.

1. National socialism and sex. 2. Concentration camp inmates—
Germany—Sexual behavior. 3. Jews—Germany—Sexual
behavior. 4. Holocaust, Jewish (1939-1945)—
Psychological aspects. 5. Eugenics—Germany—
History—20th century. 6. Holocaust, Jewish
(1939-1945) —Personal narratives. 7. Holocaust
survivors—Germany—Interviews. I. Title.

HQ18.G3F75 2002   940.53'18'019—dc21   2002040825 CIP

ISBN 0-7618-2463-4 (paperback : alk. ppr.)

The paper used in this publication meets the minimum
requirements of American National Standard for Information
Sciences—Permanence of Paper for Printed Library Materials,
ANSI Z39.48—1984

Contents

Introduction

In his writing, Michel Foucault searched for power in the most uncompromising places. Here, in this study, I am venturing into similar territory—the matrix of sexuality, but in perhaps the most uncompromising and problematic context—the Holocaust. The questions bound to arise from such a beginning are as obvious as they are disingenuous. Why focus on a topic that is so controversial and potentially offensive? Does an analysis of gender and sexuality distort historicity and defile Holocaust memory and memorialization? I believe that while these questions raise serious issues, especially as they relate to the misuse of Holocaust history for political agendas, identities, and mythologies, they do not provide sufficient justification for avoiding a discussion of what is an undeniably central element of human existence, namely sexuality, and what, more importantly, offers to add texture to the lives and deaths of survivors and victims of Nazi oppression.

The problem of embarking on such a topic is compounded by the lack of viable models and precedents in scholarly literature. Even the groundbreaking monographs on survivor psychology by Bruno Bettelheim, Terence Des Pres, and Viktor Frankl discount or distort issues of sexuality while restricting their analysis essentially to the concentration camps. For instance, Bettelheim's contention in *The Informed Heart* is that "virtually every prisoner was afraid of becoming impotent and was tempted by the anxiety to verify his potency. That meant either homosexual practices or masturbation. Prisoners indulged in both; a minority, in the first, an overwhelming majority in the second, but only rarely, and then less for enjoyment than to be sure they had not yet grown impotent."[1] Bettelheim goes on to say that the "dread of becoming impotent was closely related to infantile castration anxiety, a fear revived by SS threats of castration."[2]   In perhaps his most perplexing statement, he concludes that "old prisoners envied the newcomers' virility, and the fact that newcomers had recently enjoyed sexual experiences they themselves had been deprived of for years...By telling newcomers that all prisoners in the camp are emasculated [the old prisoners implied] that just as they had lost their virility and become impotent to revolt, so would the newcomer."[3]

In their accounts, Terence Des Pres, professor of English Literature at Colgate University, and Viktor Frankl, like Bettelheim a survivor and psychologist, argue that consensual sex among prisoners was atypical:

> [from Des Pres] One of the striking things about the concentration camp experience—and there is enormous evidence on this point—is that under conditions of privation and horror, the need for sex disappears. It simply is not there, neither in feeling nor in fantasy, neither the desire nor the drive...The fact would seem to be that when men and women are exhausted and starving, sex is not important, and that it likewise tends to be absent when the threat of death becomes constant. A momentary brush with death may very well intensify sexual desire, but when dread becomes prolonged and seeps to the core of one's being, the capacity for erotic fulfillment is ruined. Perhaps, too, disappearance of sexual desire in the camps was a biological phenomenon in service of collective survival. For if a state of nature had prevailed, men and women fighting among themselves for sexual privilege, the kind of community which grew up among prisoners would have been more difficult and open to betrayal. And it would seem, finally, that the most powerful depressors of sexual need are horror and moral disgust...Sexual joy is one of life's chief blessings, and the biological drive which enforces it is very strong. Even eros begins to govern human behavior only after a critical level of safety and well-being has been attained. If this runs counter to Freud's view—that civilized rather than primitive conditions repress erotic need—so be it. Behavior which does not support day-to-day existence tends to vanish in extremity. We may fairly conclude that what remains is indispensable.[4]

> [From Frankl]: Undernourishment, besides being the cause of the general preoccupation with food, probably also explains the

fact that the sexual urge was generally absent. Apart from the initial effects of shock, this appears to be the only explanation of a phenomenon which a psychologist was bound to observe in those all-male camps: that, as opposed to all other strictly male establishments—such as army barracks—there was little sexual perversion. Even in his dreams the prisoner did not seem to concern himself with sex, although his frustrated emotions and his finer, higher feelings did find definite expression in them. With the majority of the prisoners, the primitive life and the effort of having to concentrate on just saving one's skin led to a total disregard of anything not serving that purpose, and explained the prisoners' complete lack of sentiment.[5]

Yet even Des Pres acknowledges that sex was possible for many camp inmates, mainly kapos and cooks, men and women safer and better fed. He also grants that in places like Buchenwald and Auschwitz, the SS set up brothels, although his conclusion on the reason for this ("to dissipate the growing strength of the political underground") is questionable.[6]

Written accounts of survivors are often similarly vague, contradictory, or unreliable in their descriptions, and there is as yet no systematic investigation of sexuality during the Holocaust from the perspective of survivors who have given oral testimonies. Because of this, I have utilized as my primary source hundreds of catalogued video interviews from the Survivors of the Shoah Visual History Foundation (Steven Spielberg's Los Angeles based project.) There are approximately 50,000 testimonies in the entire archive, but, at the time of my research (1998-2000), only 3000 had been catalogued or indexed, that is, broken down into segments searchable by subjects. As a historian at the Foundation, I was able to have a degree of access to these interviews that other scholars and researchers will not have for years.

Although I examined mainly English and German language interviews conducted in the United States, Canada, England, Australia, Germany, Austria, and Israel, the testimonies reflect a broad spectrum of survivor experience and place of origin. (Most of the survivors were Polish-Jewish women, and most were teenagers when the war began.) More importantly, because in-depth questions about gender and sexuality were built in to the interviewing process, these testimonies richly address a wide array of issues such as pregnancy and birth, abortion and infanticide, menstruation, homosexual activity, consensual sex, courtships, weddings, marriages, intermarriages, divorce, sexual molestation, rape, and compulsory sterilization. As a result, I cannot conclude that sex was an unimportant facet of life under Nazi rule. Sexual conduct was pervasive—whether it was among Jews, between Jew and non-Jews, among prisoners in camps or between inmates and camp officials, between individuals in the ghettos, in hiding, or in resistance groups, or in the form prostitution. Sex as a specifically romantic and survival act in the camps was also more frequent than Des Pres and Frankl have acknowledged. The Foundation's interviews make abundantly clear that sex was an ever-present element of the prevailing power dynamic, at once exploited by many men and some women in positions of authority, and exchanged by the victims, again both men and women, to sate more immediate needs, such as hunger, self-worth, and self-preservation.

Holocaust Testimonies:
Literary, Psychological, Historical Perspectives

Oral history as a source present scholars with a particular set of difficulties. The American linguist Benjamin Lee Whorf once said that "thinking is most mysterious." In the same vein, one could describe memory as the most mysterious type of thinking. It is at once an ability and an object, a tool for conjuring images of the past and the product of that past. As a uniquely human faculty, memory is a conduit for language, ideas, metaphors, and history, as well as a window into our capacity to imagine, reify, and order disparate experiences. Memory is also hazy tapestry, often anarchic montage that when conveyed orally might tell a story or paint a picture; or it might take on a reality different from itself; or it might deceive, intentionally or not. It is often difficult, for instance, to describe a dream accurately, if at all, because images, time, and space created in dreamlike states fail to abide by coherent rules that language can capture and describe. Memory, like the individuals possessing it, is at its core, utterly dependent on a person's capabilities to remember and communicate. And memory, like its human parents, degrades over time.

It is because memories are fleeting that many scholars treat oral histories, the products of individual and collective memory, as at best problematic, at worst invalid. To historians weaned on years of study of written text, oral history is a dangerous mixture of hindsight and half-truths, distortions and omissions. Defenders of oral history could remind their detractors of similar biases in written material or indicate that contemporaneity is no guarantee of correctness. But they cannot and should not stop there. They must present a case *for* oral history, one that demonstrates not only inherent worth in capturing individual memories for posterity, but epistemological value as well. I would argue that human memories are informative both linguistically and psychologically, and, from the point of view of a historian, frequently challenge prevailing narrative consensus.

Memory, for experts in the fields of literary criticism and cultural anthropology, is a logical point of inquiry, given their core assumptions that knowledge is based upon and transmitted by language and that language itself is a series of codes that are given meaning through perception, cognition, and recollection, and conditioned by learning processes and historical context. As historian Hayden White has said: "The historically real, the past real, is that to which I can be referred only by way of an artifact that is textual in nature."[7] Oral history is a form of historical text on numerous planes and in numerous dimensions. Unlike written documents, it can be seen, heard, read as a transcript, or even remade and refashioned, for we know that no story is ever told the same way twice. Oral history is therefore distinguishable as a source from written documentation both because of its form and the mutable nature of human imagination and language.

Because testimony is a medium of communication, the slightest variation in retelling can shift meaning and significance. The words chosen to describe events, places, and people, the questions asked or not asked, the way in which questions are asked, the chemistry between interviewer and interviewee—are all locked in a moment of time. In testimony, there is a conscious and subconscious array of decisions and relationships, a prioritization of what to ask, when to ask, how to answer, what to say, what to leave out, how to say it, how to remember. According to social anthropologist Elizabeth Tonkin, "the mental registration of an event is itself an event. These registrations are so many and so hard to pin down, that it is tempting to set them apart from critical analysis. But it is misleading to do so, since they are formative of history in all its sense—action and report. There are strong arguments that the flux of life is not in itself demarcated into events. It is the subject who registers them as structure and discrete."[8] Lawrence Langer, writing on Holocaust testimonies, puts it this way:

"Oral survivor testimony unfolds before our eyes and ears; we are present at the invention of what, when we speak of written texts, we call style."[9]

For the historian, oral histories are a legitimate source precisely because they are a human rendering of the past. Survivor testimonies reposition the discussion of the Holocaust as a human event, a human catastrophe, with real people as victims, not as an abstraction of ideology or policy. Survivor accounts enrich the portrait of everyday life and death under Nazism, and they demonstrate how traumatic memory is conveyed, and how trauma can or cannot be integrated into life after the Holocaust. As Oren Baruch Stier maintains:

> Because they [video testimonies] show us 'live' images of the survivors in the 'present,' they restore to presence, life, and wholeness the 'canonical' images of skeletal survivors in striped uniforms barely alive, rehumanizing the static, lifeless, images from the past that continue to haunt us...[they also] establish a new agenda for Holocaust memorialization...The survivor speaks...directly to us, and asks us to remember her story. And, equally important, we, in watching her testimony, enter her frame of reference and in some small way, attempt to understand the horrors she witnessed. The mediating process of Holocaust video testimonies thus continues: the making of memory is an ongoing collective, communal, and cultural process that, like the memory of the survivors, never really comes to closure."[10]

Langer also contends that although historians "have the option of rejecting such testimony as a form of history," they "face the challenge of enlarging our notion of what history may be, what the Holocaust has made it, and how it urges us to reconsider the relation of past to present...."[11]

One of the more legitimate charges levied against Holocaust oral histories in the past has been their tendency to impose chronology and meaning on an event the fundamentally defies both. Again, as Oren Stier explains:

> Most of the time, survivors' stories begin with some words about their families and lives before the war, often moving soon thereafter to accounts of the circumstances under which the Nazi era first affected their own lives. For many of the

accounts, this is followed by descriptions of deportations, of ghetto life, of separating from family members, of entering the camps. After descriptions of experiences in the camps, most tell of liberation, of journeys back to hometowns to try to find family members, of leaving Europe...[12]

As Stier suggests, however, "testimony is rarely conveyed so smoothly, or with such regularity. Rather, we are witnesses to a journey over a bumpy and textured terrain of memory that each person traverses individually..."[13] According to Langer, a result of what he terms "common" memory, "with its talk of normalcy amid chaos, is to mediate atrocity, to reassure us that in spite of the ordeal some human bonds were inviolable...but simultaneously deep memory, often in the same testimony, burrows beneath the surface of the narrative to excavate episodes that corrode the comforts of common memory. Remembering and recording what happened operate on several levels, leaving atrocity and order in a permanently disrupted suspension."[14]

Those examining and conducting interviews of Holocaust survivors would be well advised to heed the charge of historian Dominick LaCapra, who believes that historians need to rethink the categories of historical understanding in order to find the "submerged" voices that contest their historical desire for unified, unambiguous meaning. That need not rule out acknowledging the ability of the survivor to "work through" the multiple traumas endured during the Holocaust. It requires only that we recognize the "irreducibility" of the loss while granting and engaging a process of mourning to enable the survivor to begin, "however self-questioningly and haltingly," a limited renewal of life.[15]

When survivors speak of sex in oral testimonies, however, they are not always analytical, and they invite listeners into a concentric circle of intimacy. One must be ever sensitive to this, for the pain pervading testimony about mass murder is compounded by revelations about the most personal and vulnerable aspect of one's humanity. In many of their Shoah Foundation interviews, survivors are for the first time confronting aspects of their wartime trauma that involved sexual and intimate experiences. This frank and public discussion of sexuality in many respects complicates the picture by crossing a psychoanalytical threshold; survivors take what is most often buried subtext and elevate it to the level of text. One way to reassure survivors of the importance of a scholarly endeavor dealing with sex and at the same time to get at the subtext behind sexual discourse, would be to couple discussions of sexuality with questions about the social construction of memory. By investigating potential differences in *how* survivors recount their most intimate memories through sociological prisms such as gender, we might gain understanding on several fronts: what mechanisms enabled some victims to survive, what types of survivor personalities were able to speak of sex, how were survivors able to cope with physical brutality that involved sexual abuse, how did women's experiences and perceptions of those experiences differ from men, how did the experiences and perceptions of adults differ from those of children, and so on. How a survivor encodes sex through language should also be of prime interest and importance to the historian. To quote psychologist and researcher Henry Greenspan, "...survivors retell more than specific incidents they witnessed and endured. They also convey what it is to *be* a survivor...In the course of recounting, such self-presentations emerge in various ways: in survivors' direct reflections about who they are and what they have become; in the narrative identity each assumes while retelling; and, most implicitly, in the tones and cadences of their speech..."[16]

Current research on the experiences of women during the Holocaust has laid the groundwork for a more extensive investigation of sexuality and sexual behavior. Consider as examples Marlene Heinemann's findings that "sexual abuse and ordinary camp labor were two intertwined aspects of the female deportees experience,[17] and the similar conclusions of Dalia Ofer, Joan Ringelheim, and Lenore Weitzman.[18] The three essays in this manuscript take their focus even further and make a singular contribution to Holocaust and gender studies by exploring survivor testimony for memories of sexual politics and the functioning of the Nazi state, sexual abuse that often cut across gender lines, and sexual behavior in the different contexts of persecution—ghettos, camps, and hiding. Examining the testimonies of homosexuals, children of mixed marriages, and individuals who were subject to sterilization, the first article confronts the extent to which sexuality through eugenic ideology shaped Nazi racial ideology and policies. The second essay explores gender-related issues such as pregnancy, menstruation, rape, and sexual concealment—issues that often constituted central experiences of Jewish women and men as victims of Nazi persecution. The final essay focuses more closely on the remembrance of sexual behavior during the Holocaust and the degree to which sexuality was an element of survival or an additional burden of trauma and degradation in the "deep" memory of survivors.

Notes

[1] Bruno Bettelheim, *The Informed Heart: Autonomy in a Mass Age* (New York, 1960), 195, 196.

[2] Ibid.

[3] Ibid.

[4] Terence Des Pres, *The Survivor* (New York, 1976), 189-191.

[5] Viktor Frankl, *Man's Search for Meaning* (New York, 1952), 52.

[6] Des Pres, 190

[7] Hayden White, *The Content of the Form: Narrative Discourse and Historical Representation* (Baltimore, 1987), 186.

[8] Elizabeth Tonkin, *Narrating Our Pasts: The Social Construction of Oral History* (Cambridge, 1992), 120.

[9] Lawrence Langer, *Holocaust Testimonies: The Ruins of Memory* (Yale, 1991), 58.

[10] Oren Baruch Stier, "Framing the Witness: The Memorial Role of Holocaust Video Testimonies," in John Roth and Elisabeth Maxwell, eds., *Remembering for the Future: The Holocaust in an Age of Genocide* (New York, 2001), 202, 203.

[11] Langer, 57.

[12] Baruch Stier, 192

[13] Ibid.

[14] Langer, 9

[15] Saul Friedländer has a less optimistic outlook: "It may well be that for some the trauma, the insuperable moral outrage, the riddle whose decoding never seems to surrender a fully comprehensible text, may present an ongoing emotional and intellectual challenge. However, I would venture to suggest that even if new forms of historical narrative were to develop, or new modes of representation, and even if literature and art were to probe the past from unexpected vantage points, the opaqueness of some 'deep memory' would probably not be dispelled. 'Working through' may ultimately signify, in Maurice Blanchot's words, 'to keep watch over absent meaning.' Friedländer, "Trauma, Transference, and 'Working Through' in Writing the History of the Shoah, *History and Memory* 4/1 (Spring/Summer 1992): 55, as cited in Gertrud Koch, "'Against All Odds' or the Will to Survive," *History and Memory* 9/1 and 2 (1997): 395, 296; Dominick LaCapra, *Representing the Holocaust: History, Theory, Trauma* (Cornell, 1994), 193, 199, and *History and Memory After Auschwitz* (Ithaca, 1998), 110.

[16] Henry Greenspan, *On Listening to Holocaust Survivors* (Westport, Conn., 1998), 15.

[17] Marlene Heinemann, *Gender and Destiny: Women Writers and the Holocaust* (Westport, Conn., 1986), 18.

[18] Dalia Ofer and Lenore Weitzman, eds., *Women in the Holocaust* (New Haven, 1998); Joan Ringelheim, "The Holocaust: Taking Women into Account," *Jewish Quarterly* (Autumn 1992): 19-23; Carol Rittner, and John Roth, eds. *Different Voices: Women and the Holocaust* (St. Paul, Minnesota, 1993).

Chapter 1

The "Eugenic Utopia"

Nazism was a multi-headed hydra of evil, but one of its core strands was a particular scientific and sexual vision of utopia that had its origins in the theories of eugenicists or racial hygienists who, in the late 19th century, had refashioned the solutions to contemporary social problems in biological terms. The term eugenics, meaning good birth, was coined in 1883 by the British naturalist Francis Galton. Its premise was simple: breed more of the white, educated, middle and upper classes, cut off the reproductive capacities of practically everyone else. This recasting of traditional bigotry through the idiom of procreation occurred in the context of Darwin's theory of the survival of the fittest, early breakthroughs in genetics, and anthropological surveys that placed white European males at the pinnacle of human achievement.

Science and eugenics were an almost too perfect pair; eugenics allowed scientists to vent their frequent economic frustrations and prejudices against the "other" in a manner that not only befit the educated patriarchy of the middle class but also provided an air of "enlightened" authority to that hatred. Eugenics both reflected strong anxieties over crime, poverty, disease, and urban ethnic mixing and legitimized an otherwise irrational desire to control, subjugate, and in many instances, eliminate innocent people of different abilities, classes, ethnicities, races, and genders. Thus, by exerting influence over public policy and social discourse in the 19th century, many professionals within the life and social sciences laid the groundwork for a 20th century mindset that was questionable in its commitment to individual rights, and yet seemingly incontestable in its empiricism.

"Positive Eugenics" in the Third Reich

The guiding metaphors of Nazism were that the Germans were a superior "race" linked by "blood" and that Germany's woes resulted from decades of racial degradation. The only solution to these problems was a wholesale purging of "parasitic" and "worthless" agents. Racial theory shaped the Nazi party platform of 1920, most notably in point four where German ancestry was to be the main prerequisite for citizenship, and Hitler made crude assumptions about race, genetics, and fertility in his many diatribes on racial conflict in *Mein Kampf.* To cite a few examples:

> The German Reich as a state...has the task, not only of assembling and preserving the most valuable stocks of basic racial elements in this people, but slowly and surely raising them to a dominant position...[1]

> Every racial crossing leads inevitably sooner or later to the decline of the hybrid product...[2]

> The folkish state must make up for what everyone else today has neglected in this field. It must set race in the center of all life. It must take care to keep it pure. It must declare the child to be the most precious treasure of the people. It must see to it that only the healthy beget children...[3]

> Those who are physically and mentally unhealthy and unworthy must not perpetuate their suffering in the body of their children.[4]

An associated complaint feeding the Nazi obsession about population was that the "two-child" family was breeding Germany's "Aryan" population out of existence. A fear of "organic" or "biological" degeneration had pervaded the German public consciousness since the turn of the century, when demographic realities stemming from industrialization and urbanization were effecting smaller population growth. The fear of *Volkstod*, or "People's Death," grew exponentially as a result of the devastating losses suffered by Germany in World War I. Although Germany was continuing to experience growth, albeit at a lower rate, demographic propagandists and scientists with dubious motives, chiefly psychiatrists, anthropologists, and biologists, began to suggest that "good" German stock was being overrun by degenerates of all types—by racial "degenerates" (i.e., Jews) and hereditary "degenerates" (the mentally and physically handicapped and those with physical diseases such as tuberculosis and venereal diseases.) In 1900, the German birthrate stood at thirty-six births per one thousand people, but by 1932, it had plunged to fifteen per thousand.[5] A eugenic view of women fit into the Nazi framework accordingly:

[from soon to be Propaganda Minister, Joseph Goebbels:] The woman has the task of being pretty and of brining children into the world.[6]

[from professor of racial hygiene Fritz Lenz—back in 1913]: Now it is a fact that a woman is capable of giving birth for a period of nearly thirty years. Even when we consider a woman giving birth only once every two years, this means a minimum of fifteen births per mother. Anything less that this must be considered the result of unnatural or pathological causes.[7]

The process of molding the Nazi utopia therefore entailed 1) the promotion of a greater birth rate among "Aryan" mothers 2) the prevention of such births by those deemed to be hereditarily "unfit" and 3) the concomitant prevention of any sexual intermingling between "Aryans" and "inferior races" (aimed essentially at Jews.) The Nazis quickly began crafting their new eugenic order within a few months of Hitler's appointment as chancellor in 1933.

On the "promotion" end, the Nazis passed laws intended to lure working women back into the home. They offered loans to married men (ranging from 500 to 1000RM) if their wives would agree to stop working in the public sphere, and as an additional incentive, they arranged for the loan principal to be reduced by one-quarter for each child born. By February 1936, Nazi officials had awarded over 500,000 loans valued at more than 300 million RM.[8] At the same time that they were vigorously advancing their "mother-as-breeder" agenda, the Nazis began agitating for a more ruthless enforcement of existing anti-abortion laws. Viewing abortion, among fit "Aryan" women only, as a crime against the "race," they sought to cut down on both illegal operations and those conducted for medical reasons that were technically legal, cases of ectopic pregnancies for instance. (One Nazi health official estimated that doctors performed close to half a million illicit abortions in 1933 alone.)[9] Draconian police methods resulted in a drop in the number of abortion applications from over 40,000 in 1932 to barely over 14,000 for the entire period between 1935 and 1940.[10]

"Negative Eugenics:" The Sterilization Law

Among the first Nazi laws to restrict a group of people on eugenic and hereditarian grounds was the Law for the Prevention of Hereditarily Diseased Offspring, passed on July 14, 1933. This law called for the compulsory sterilization of any individual suffering from the following illnesses: inherited "feeblemindedness," schizophrenia, manic-depression, epilepsy, congenital blindness and deafness, and chronic alcoholism. Between January 1, 1934, when the law went into effect and 1939, the Nazis succeeded in sterilizing approximately 400,000 individuals, mostly those diagnosed as mildly "feebleminded," but living outside of mental institutions and hence regarded as dangerous because their sexual relationships could not easily be regulated. The procedures involved in sterilization were, usually, tubal ligation for women and vasectomy for men, operations that were hardly routine for the time and resulted in the deaths of over two thousand individuals, mainly women.

It is important to note that the history of sterilization in Germany did not begin with the Nazis. One of Germany's leading psychiatrists and co-author of the 1933 law, Ernst Rüdin, had advocated sterilizing alcoholics as early as 1903, and in 1929, he wrote that mental illness could be predicted and averted by sterilization.[11] Fritz Lenz reinforced the academic campaign by arguing that eugenic sterilization did not constitute criminal assault.[12] The preface to the racial hygiene journal *Eugenik, Erblehre, und Erbpflege* had this to say:

> A crushing and ever growing burden of useless individuals unworthy of life is maintained and taken care of in institutions at the expense of the healthy—of whom thousands are today without their own place to live and millions of whom starve from lack of work. Does not today's predicament cry out strongly enough for a planned economy, i.e., eugenics, in health policy?[13]

For his part, Otto Kankeleit, in a 1929 monograph, *Sterilization for Racial Hygienic and Social Reasons*, discussed the various methods of sterilization, ranging from castration to vasectomy and tubal ligation, and, more importantly, identified the very groups that would later be targeted by the 1933 law.   Support for sterilization before Hitler's appointment as chancellor cut across the political spectrum. In 1928, Social Democrats supported sterilizing "hereditarily ill criminals" as the precondition for their release from prison, a measure which had the support of the Nazi Party.[14] Also that same year, eugenicist Rainer Fetscher, a left-leaning liberal doctor and author of numerous texts on eugenics for the Dresden Hygiene Museum, began performing unauthorized and illegal sterilizations.   In the summer of 1932, a draft of a voluntary sterilization bill came out of the Prussian Health Council. Seventy-eight individuals, nearly half of them medical experts, took part in the sessions drafting the law, including Nazi doctor Leonardo Conti, and prominent eugenicists Erwin Baur, Eugen Fischer, and Otmar Freiherr von Verschuer.   By and large, the German medical community supported the bill. Only the Catholic Church, following the 1930 papal encyclical "Casti Connubii" condemned the practice. On December 10, the issue came before the Reich Ministry of Interior, and the medical chamber of Prussia demanded a decision one way or another on the proposal. Administrators were, in words of historian Paul Weindling, taken over by the political events of January 1933.[15]

Sterilization as a matter of state policy was not limited to Germany either. Danish officials passed a sterilization law in 1929, and other Scandinavian countries, compelled less by racial than social motives, passed sterilization laws of their own in the mid-thirties (Norway in 1934, Sweden and Finland in 1935, Iceland in 1938). The most prominent model for sterilization legislation was the United States, where, by 1939 more than 30,000 individuals had been sterilized—mostly patients in mental institutions in California.

What the Nazis did was to take previous discussions and proposals for sterilization and radicalize them. After the 1933 law, every German doctor was expected to register patients with relevant illnesses and then apply to have them sterilized. These applications were then to be reviewed by special courts, so-called Hereditary Health Courts, nearly two hundred of which were established. Composed of a lawyer and two doctors, one of whom specialized in heredity and genetic pathology, these courts ruled in favor of sterilization in the vast majority of cases brought before them. The first "genetic health" court met on 15 March 1934 in Berlin; it heard 348 cases and ordered 325 sterilizations. In 1934 alone, Hereditary Health Courts handed down nearly 65,000 decisions; 56,000 were in favor of sterilization. Of the seven percent who appealed (nearly 4,000 cases), only 377 were successful in overturning the lower court ruling. Augmenting the place of the Hereditary Health Court in German state and society was the 18 October 1935 passage of the Law for the Protection of the Hereditary Health of the German People, which mandated anyone seeking a marriage license to obtain a certificate of "genetic" health from his or her doctor. This particular piece of legislation emerged in the wake of the series of racial decrees that became known as the Nuremberg Laws, which I will discuss later in this chapter.

The sterilization program, too, was not immune from a racial application. In 1937, some 500 children of mixed parentage, half African, half German, were forcibly sterilized by the Nazis in the name of "racial purification." The fathers of these children were African soldiers in the French army who had served as part of the Allied force occupying sections of western Germany along the Rhine river after World War I. Detractors of the occupation likened the presence of blacks to a "curse" and dubbed the children of black soldiers and German women, "Rhineland Bastards." In *Mein Kampf*, Hitler spared no hatred for these children: "The contamination by Negro blood on the Rhine in the heart of Europe is just as much in keeping with the perverted sadistic thirst for vengeance of this hereditary enemy of our people as is the ice cold calculation of the Jew thus to begin bastardizing the European continent at its core and to deprive the white race of the foundations for a sovereign existence through infection with lower humanity…"[16]

The first measure taken against Afro-Germans under the Nazis came in April 1933 when Hermann Göring, as Prussian Minister of the Interior, requested authorities in Düsseldorf, Cologne, Koblenz, and Aachen to provide statistical information on the racially mixed children. That same year, Dr. Hans Macco published a pamphlet entitled "Racial Problems in the Third Reich," in which he advocated sterilizing all "half-castes" and Gypsies. Yet it was not until 1935 that serious discussions began concerning the fate of the Rhineland children. In the commentaries on the Nuremberg Laws, Blacks were, for the first time, grouped together as a matter of law with Jews and Gypsies, making them ineligible for higher rights of citizenship. Initially, the Nazis used the term "non-Aryan" to take away rights from those who did not have "German blood." But the term was too broad, potentially affecting and angering a wide group of ethnicities the Nazis later needed to placate—such as Chinese, Indian, Japanese, and even Arab nationals living in Germany. Conversely, the focus of the Nuremberg Laws solely on Jews was too narrow, necessitating further commentary on other groups that should be disenfranchised—namely, Gypsies and Blacks.

In March 1935, a Reich Council for Population and Racial Policy met to discuss sterilizing Afro-German children. Presiding over the meeting were Ernst Rüdin and Arthur Gütt of the Department of Public Health within the Reich Ministry of Interior. Also present were Fritz Lenz, Walter Gross (head of the Nazi Racial Policy Office), and Gerhard Wagner (Reich Doctors' Leader). Both racial hygienists, Lenz and Rüdin, supported forcibly expelling the children, while party ideologues Gross and Wagner pushed for a radical sterilization plan that was to be both compulsory and secret. Moreover, they insisted that Hitler himself decide the issue. By 1937, it was decided to sterilize all Afro-German children outside of the law. It is not known whether Hitler issued direct orders to that effect. Nevertheless, the sterilizations that followed were technically illegal because under the 1933 Sterilization Law, only individuals with hereditary "defects" were to be targeted. There were no specific "racial" provisions, and the law was not intended to apply to Jews or Gypsies.[17]

At the beginning of 1937, the Gestapo formed Special Commission No. 3 with subcommissions in Wiesbaden, Ludwigshafen, and Koblenz, which included public health officials and academic experts. The latter helped locate Afro-German children, examine them for their racial background, and hand them over to designated hospitals. Among the experts were Wolfgang Abel, Engelhardt Bühler, Herbert Göllner, and Heinrich Schade. The children investigated by Schade were taken to the Institute for Hereditary Biology and Racial Hygiene in Frankfurt, headed by leading racial hygienist Otmar Verschuer. There, they were subjected to series of anthropometric measurements and then sent off to a hospital to be sterilized. In one instance, Eugen Fischer, the head of the Kaiser Wilhelm Institute for Anthropology, Eugenics, and Human Heredity, conducted the physical examination himself.[18]

The sterilization program proper ended with the sixth decree implementing the law, which prohibited all sterilizations after August 31, 1939. By then, the Nazis had adopted a murderous policy to deal with the mentally and physically handicapped. Investigations over the suitability of marriages were also discontinued as doctors were needed for the war effort. However, sterilizations would continue in the form of deadly experiments visited upon concentration camp inmates. The methods of sterilization would become more insidious as well. In 1935, Nazi officials had sanctioned abortions for "unfit" mothers and "voluntary" castration for gay men. Less than a year later, Nazi health authorities passed an amendment to the Sterilization Law permitting the use of X-rays to sterilize women over the age of the thirty-eight or women for whom tubal ligation might prove risky. During the war, SS chief Heinrich Himmler suggested experimenting with different techniques. Dr. Carl Clauberg heeded the call and was responsible for sterilizing several thousand women at the infamous Block 10 in Auschwitz by injecting toxic chemicals into their uteruses.

It is ironic that Clauberg, a gynecologist in Königshütte who wrote his dissertation on female sex hormones and worked at the Kiel University Clinic on producing a synthetic hormone that would aid in pregnancy, came to dedicate his research to an entirely opposite goal. Promising Himmler a method of sterilization that was not invasive, Clauberg maintained that with injection, he could sterilize one thousand women per day with minimal complications. Beginning in 1942, he initiated his experiment, enlisting nearly seven hundred female prisoners from Birkenau. Vaginally injecting such toxins as barium sulfate, silver nitrate, and novocaine, he concluded that the "benefits" of such a procedure were outweighed by the disadvantages of toxicity, especially the often fatal side effects of fever and infection. X-Rays continued to be explored, however, and in Block 30, nearly one thousand men and women between the ages of seventeen to twenty-five were exposed to high doses for several minutes at a time.[19]

In the remembrances below, survivors of the Nazi eugenics program confront a pervasive fear, disbelief, and lack of knowledge surrounding their fates, as well as the physical and emotion pain suffered as a consequence of their "operations." Some lament the loss of identity, a specific German identity that had been tenuous from the start, while for others, it is the robbing of their sexuality that is as unforgivable as it is ineffaceable.

Born in Frankfurt in August 1920, Johann H. was one of the children the Germans dubbed "Rheinland Bastarde" because he came from mixed parentage. His mother was German, but his father was an Algerian soldier in the French Army who served as part of the Rhineland occupying force. Teased by his schoolmates, Johann usually played the role of the French soldier in playground games. In his testimony, he is blunt about his childhood: "I was the living proof of the German defeat. I would not have existed if Germany had won."[20] In 1928, following the death of his mother, Johann was taken in by his grandmother.

During the sterilization action against the Rhineland children, Johann was identified by Gestapo officials and taken to a hospital to have a vasectomy, although he was left unaware of his destination. "I was afraid…I had no idea what was going to happen."[21] The operation lasted forty minutes. Johann remembers little of the procedure, except that it was painful. He insists that his surgeons were friendly and even gave him two bottles of beer to help him recover more quickly. The fact remained, however, that Johann did not know what to do afterwards. He was simply told he could not marry anyone with German or "related blood" because he himself was no longer regarded as German or "related blood."[22]

Klara N., born in Berlin in March 1921, was sterilized not because of her race, but because the Nazis alleged that she suffered from hereditary schizophrenia. In the fall of 1939, Klara's brother was diagnosed as schizophrenic, sent to a psychiatric clinic, and eventually transferred to the Charite hospital in Berlin. Klara discovered after the war that her brother was suffering from rheumatic fever, which would have explained the feverish hallucinations he was having, and she believes to this day that his physical illness was a pretext for a psychiatric diagnosis. When Klara tried to visit her brother at the hospital, she herself was detained and eventually sterilized. In 1941, she was summoned to appear before one of the many Hereditary Health Courts established throughout Germany after the passage of the 1933 Sterilization Law. In her brief, ten minute hearing, the court gave Klara the choice of remaining in the psychiatric hospital or undergoing a tubal ligation as a precondition for her release. She chose the latter. "It was very stressful for me…there was no ambulance, I had a short recovery period…"[23]

After the war, Klara was determined to right the injustice she and so many like her suffered. Initially rebuffed by the West German government, which did not regard her forcible sterilization as subject to restitution, Klara formed in 1986 the Union of Victims of the Euthanasia and Forced Sterilization Programs. The organization would eventually boast a membership of nearly eight hundred individuals. In 1988, West German officials offered Klara a meager 5,000

Deutschmarks as compensation, but only if she acknowledged that this would satisfy her claim and end all future claims.[24] Her statement at the end of her testimony demonstrates how inconsequential money actually was in the entire equation: "We can have no joy over children or grandchildren...We don't have this...We don't have a successor generation...A generation to raise and support..."[25]

Jack O. was born Jacob Skurnik on May 10, 1924 in Sierpc, Poland, one of six children in his Orthodox Jewish home. During the war, he was deported to Auschwitz, where he was separated from his family and placed with thirty-five to forty other prisoners in a special "sterilization" program. "A Polish doctor, [Wladislaw] Dering performed the castration. I lay there naked. When he cut into my flesh, I remember those words, you 'goddamn Jew, If you make one more sound, I'll make sure you don't get off this bed.' There was bleeding, bleeding, the blood became yellow and green. I even put my own urine to it. After six months, it finally showed signs of healing. I was called out again to go through the procedure on the other side. I don't know how the hell I survived..."[26]

Jack was fifteen when he underwent the operation. "I did not know. I did not know the consequences. I was laying on the bunk. The doctor gave me a shot, but the doctor must have enjoyed what he was doing. The shot didn't kill the pain. He cut in the front. To me it was a downgrading. I'm glad I was able to come out alive. This did happen. I have the scars to prove it. I saw my father one more time walking by and he heard about it and asked if it was true. We never had a word in our language for castration on humans. Only when referring to fixing horses. That was the last time I saw my father. Quite a few other boys went the operation. Forty. Only three or four of us are left in the whole world."[27] In February 1945, Jack was liberated by Soviet forces—but he was able to make his way to the American zone, where he learned how to operate motion picture film projectors. Shortly thereafter, he immigrated to the United States.

The Persecution of Homosexuals

A corollary to the Nazi fixation with better breeding was the desire to root out homosexuality, again among "Aryans," because of its demographic implications. As with their campaign against abortion, the Nazis stepped up enforcement of existing laws against same-sex behavior (paragraph 175 of the German Penal Code of 1871) and added broader categories and more severe sentences (so that even glances were punishable). The original paragraph 175 targeted males who indulged "in criminally indecent activity with another male, or who [allow themselves] to participate in such activity. The Nazi revision of 1935 inserted a provision against activity encompassing "any form of criminal indecency between men or behavior likely to offend public morality or arouse sexual desire in oneself or strangers." It is estimated that between 1933 and 1939, nearly 15,000 German homosexual men were put into concentration camps for violating paragraph 175.

Yet there was some tension among Nazi officials and eugenicists with regard to their beliefs in both the origins of homosexuality and its racial hygienic impact. This ideological dilemma, which was never truly resolved, pitted a biological view of homosexuality against a behavioral one. Many physicians argued that homosexuals posed a threat to public health and regularly described homosexuality as "a pathology" and gay men as "psychopaths." Doctors writing on behalf of the Nazi Racial Policy Office characterized homosexuals as weak, unreliable, and deceitful and argued that they were so out of choice: "They are not poor sick people to be treated, but enemies of the state to be eliminated!"[28]   SS chief Heinrich Himmler used similar language, believing that homosexuals imperiled the "maintenance and strengthening of the power of the German nation."[29] In scientific publications, however, one could find arguments against persecution on the basis of genetics. The Nazi biologist and racial hygienist Theo Lang, for one, cautioned against propelling homosexuals into marriage and "normal" forms of sexuality because they would simply perpetuate their genetic "defect," echoing a similar argument made by Ernst Rüdin at the turn of the century.[30]

The problem for Nazi ideologues was obvious: If they took the position that homosexuality was the product of a genetic "flaw," forcing homosexuals to reproduce would have only made matters worse. But allowing homosexuals to pursue their inclinations, to "breed themselves out" as it were, would have run counter to the Nazi vision of masculinity. If, on the other hand, the Nazis took a behavioral approach to homosexuality, it would have undercut their belief that everything in life came down to blood and biology. Female homosexuals were by and large absent from the entire discussion, and when they were persecuted, it was not because of their sexual orientation, but for other crimes—mainly prostitution. (According to Nazi tallies, lesbians made up approximately sixty percent of all prostitutes).[31]

The contradictory impulses in Nazi thinking towards homosexuals extended to the world of the concentration camps, where, in one bizarre flight of fancy, Himmler commissioned a Danish SS Doctor, Carl Vaernet, to investigate whether homosexuality could be "cured." At Buchenwald, Vaernet implanted in 180 male prisoners hormone capsules that released excess amounts of testosterone. He concluded that this high dosage was sufficient to eradicate homosexual tendencies; in 1944, Himmler ordered Vaernet's patients visit the brothel at Ravensbrück to test the hypothesis. The fate of these patients is unknown.[32]

The concentration camp was also a world in which two homosexual realities prevailed: the widespread occurrence of situational same-sex couplings among otherwise heterosexual prisoners, something that was ignored, and the brutal treatment of homosexual prisoners. According to Heinz Heger, "The prisoners with the pink triangle were, as always, 'filthy queers' in the eyes of the other prisoners, while the very fellow prisoners who insulted and condemned us in this way were quite unperturbed by relationships that the block seniors and kapos had with the young Poles, and just smiled at this behaviour, even if somewhat ironically...Homosexual behaviour between two 'normal' men is considered an emergency outlet, while the same thing between two gay men, who both feel deeply for one another, is something 'filthy' and repulsive..."[33] Hans-Georg Stümke concurs: "Homosexuals "occupied the lowest rung in the prisoner hierarchy. In Buchenwald...they made up the highest proportion of inmates transported to the extermination camps...prisoners with the pink triangle 'never lived very long, and were rapidly and systematically eliminated by the SS.'[34]

The stories of the following gay men show the different contours of anti-homosexual persecution under the Nazis. They also illustrate the themes of burgeoning adolescent identity and early relationships as well as the condition for gay men in the concentration camps. Two of the testimonies, those of Gad B. and Peter S., reveal the extent to which diametrically opposite experiences (love in the case of Gad, abuse in the case of Peter) could have radical and strikingly similar effects on one's sexual identity.

Gad B., born in Berlin in 1923, faced the dual issue of being a half-Jew in Germany as well as a homosexual. Given his status as a so-called *Mischling*, Gad was afforded a degree of freedom, of which he took full advantage, rescuing some one hundred Jews from deportation—either by providing shelter or false identity papers. He was unable, however, to save the life of his boyfriend, Manfred. In October 1942, Manfred's family was arrested and taken away to be deported. Searching for options, Gad consulted Manfred's boss, a house painter, who suggested that Gad don his son's Hitler Youth uniform and attempt a rescue—overlooking the fact that his son was over six feet tall and Gad was only five foot three. Making his way to the transit station in this oversized uniform, Gad secured Manfred's release on the pretext that he had "hidden paint supplies and keys to apartments that needed work."[35] Yet Manfred was not able to leave his family behind. "What kind of freedom is that when I can't be with my family?" Manfred returned to the station. No-one from his family would survive the war. For Gad, the decision was a turning point. "I grew up in that moment."[36]

Unlike Gad, Stefan K., a Polish Catholic form Thorn, was unable to keep his sexual orientation hidden from the Nazis. Stefan was fourteen years old in 1939, when his town was occupied by the German army. In November 1941, a German soldier (originally from Austria) named Willi began courting Stefan. A romantic relationship ensued, and Stefan fell deeply in love. His relationship caused discomfort among friends and family, but the affair lasted only until the spring of 1942, when Willi's battalion was mobilized to the Russian front. Willi promised he would write, but he never did. Stefan, however, did send a letter laced with romantic innuendoes. Detained on 19 September 1942 by Gestapo officials who had intercepted the fateful communication, Stefan was brutally beaten and jailed for "demoralizing" a German soldier.[37]

In 1942, Erwin W., an Austrian, was thirty-three years old when he was arrested during a raid on the gay bathhouse Esterhazy. Two years later, a military court convicted him to five years in a penitentiary and discharged him from the army. Interned in the Krems-Stein prison, Erwin survived what became known as the "Bloody Friday of Stein," the massacre of inmates on 6 April 1945 carried out by SA officials fleeing Soviet forces. During the melee, Erwin was hidden by a guard: He insists: "There were also officials who felt and acted humanely." Erwin's survival did not necessarily mean release, however, and he was sent by boat to a prison in Straubing, then to Munich Stadelheim, and finally to Bernau am Chiemsee. American troops liberated Erwin from this prison in May 1946. "My imprisonment was brutal. Physically, I was very weak, and for a height of 1.77 m, I weighed only thirty-nine kilos…In the late fall of 1946, I returned to Austria and found little support from officials. I was not permitted to be re-instated to my job as a financial advisor, so I had to make due as a low-end white collar worker."[38]

Erwin's disillusionment is matched by the weariness of Peter S. Born in 1924 in Anna Paulowna, a small village in the Netherlands, Peter became involved in the Dutch resistance—as a mere teen—after the German invasion and occupation. His main duty was to forge food ration tickets and distribute them. For this, he was arrested and incarcerated in Buchenwald as a political prisoner. While in Buchenwald, Peter worked sorting clothes, a job he obtained by exchanging sexual favors. Because of his good looks, he was relentlessly pursued by fellow inmates as well as camp officials. Raped and sexually assaulted numerous times, Peter became numb to the encounters. They were, in his words, "just part of life in the camp."[39] Peter was subjected to further violations in the form of medical experiments. (He was the sole survivor of a group intentionally infected with typhus.) He also remembers that the Germans built a brothel near the hospital dubbed "The Little Camp." Some twenty women, mostly French prisoners, were put there with the promise that they would be released after six months. Each woman had her own room and bed and received three to five "customers" per night. Peter was able to obtain such detailed information on the brothel because he was the one who sewed clothes for the women. After the war, Peter married a Dutch Catholic woman and went on to raise four children, three of whom have birth defects, which he attributes to the typhus experiments he endured at Buchenwald. His marriage ended in divorce after twenty-four years; it took Peter this long to be able to confront his true sexual leanings and wartime sexual experiences, and move past the latter to pursue the openly gay lifestyle he now leads. Peter, in so many respects, embodies what Lawrence Langer terms the "diminished self" as he frequently buries his pain in mute resignation and emotional anesthesia.

The recognition of homosexuals as victims of Nazi persecution has been slow in coming, hampered by the persistence of homophobia in German state and society. It was not until the late

1960s that the infamous paragraph 175 was repealed, and it was not until 1985 that homosexuals received mention as victims from the highest symbolic office in the country, that of President. In 1999, the Sachsenhausen museum became the first memorial in Germany officially to acknowledge homosexuals as victims of Nazi persecution.[40]

Preventing Intermarriage

As the central targets of Nazi oppression, Jews saw their social and sexual freedoms curtailed in drastic fashion. While the anti-Jewish laws passed by the Nazi regime between 1933 and 1935 destroyed the professional and private lives of countless German Jews, the statutes remained vague on the actual question "who was a Jew," relying as they did on the overly diffuse concept of "non-Aryan." In addition, they did little to regulate intimate contact between Jews and non-Jews. The need for clarity on the "Jewish Question" was made acute, in the eyes of the Nazis, following an outbreak of antisemitic violence throughout German cities and towns in the summer of 1935. The Kurfürstendamm in Berlin, the city's major thoroughfare, was the site of some of the worst antisemitic rioting before Kristallnacht in 1938.

Disputes between party radicals and state bureaucrats also hastened the drive for a comprehensive measure against Jews in German society. For their part, Walter Gross of the Nazi Racial Political Office and Gerhard Wagner, Reich Doctors' Leader, two of the most strident ideologues within the Nazi Party's medical establishment, pushed for a racialization of the 1933 sterilization law, which had not been directed against Jews. Their aspirations were realized at the Nazi Party's seventh annual congress in Nuremberg in September 1935, where Wagner not only laid out justification for the subsequent murder of the handicapped[41] but paved the way for the eugenic complex of decrees that has become known simply as the Nuremberg Laws. In his speech of September 12, Wagner leveled familiar charges against Jews in Germany (that they dominated the economy, that they were cunning and manipulative, and so forth) and hinted that a law was in the works to prevent the "further bastardization" of Germany through German-Jewish intermarriage, which by 1930 neared thirty percent in some large cities like Berlin and Frankfurt, but only ten to fifteen percent in rural areas.[42]

Passed on September 15, 1935, the first law, the "Reich Citizenship Law," created a special status of citizenship for those with German or related blood, bestowing upon these "Reichsbürger" all political rights (what little was left of them). Jews (and, in later commentaries, Gypsies and "Negroes") were to be regarded as national subjects, entitled to the right to hold passports and seek protection under the law but not much else.[43] The second law, the "Law for the Protection of German Blood and Honor," prohibited German-Jewish intermarriage and sexual relations and forbade Jews from displaying the Reich colors and from employing German women under the age of forty-five, playing on the image of Jews as sexual predators.[44]

In November, a supplement to the "Blood" law cemented the distinctions between Jews, "mixed breeds" or *Mischlinge* and non-Jews. "Full" Jews were those with three or more Jewish grandparents, or those *Mischlinge* with two grandparents who either belonged to the Jewish community or who were married to a Jew. Those with two Jewish grandparents who did not belong to the Jewish community were given the designation, *Mischling* Grade One. Those with only one Jewish grandparent who did not belong to the Jewish community were designated *Mischling* Grade Two. It is estimated that only eleven percent of children from Jewish-Christian marriages in Germany remained religiously Jewish before 1933. Nazi calculations put the number of *Mischling* at between three to four hundred thousand.[45] By making it illegal to marry or consort with the newly defined Jew, the framers of the Nuremberg Laws sought to pave the way for the disappearance of all cross breeds over time.

With the passage of these two laws, the Nazis brought Jewish policy in line with their assumption s that Jews were evil "because of their blood and that their most heinous crime had been the defilement of Aryan racial purity," not the infiltration of the civil service, the various professions, or the German economy.[46] Yet the Nazis had to rely on religious affiliation and marital status to formulate a biological basis for the Jewish "race." The inability of Nazi anthropologists and eugenicists to find a distinct Jewish blood type and their reliance on overexaggerated studies of physical characteristics (of the Jewish nose, Jewish face, or Jewish posture) revealed the absurdity of their basic antisemitic suppositions.

Enforcement of the Nuremberg Laws was equally problematic and cumbersome. The statutes built on the administrative structure of the Sterilization Law and the 1934 Public Health Law, which united state and municipal health services. City officials were now required to ask questions about both genetic health and "racial" heritage, and to report suspicious applicants to the local health offices that issued the relevant "permits." Couples were to submit first to a physical exam to obtain a marital health certificate, and then, if intermarriage were at issue, obtain the permission of a special committee, The Committee for the Protection of German Blood, made up of, among others, Drs. Arthur Gütt, of the Interior Ministry, and Gerhard Wagner, the Chief Nazi Doctor. In order to keep pace with the flood of paperwork, nearly 750 new health offices were created in Germany by the beginning of 1937. That year, the central Reich Health Office in Berlin was expanded to include special divisions on marital counseling, sterilization, genetic registration, and Jewish miscegenation. But the work to be done outstripped the available resources. In February 1938, Gütt admitted in a letter to Himmler that the Reich Health Office was being overworked to the point where it could not guarantee anything but a cursory examination of applicants' racial fitness.[47]

The Nuremberg Laws also gave rise to a new category of crime, *Rassenschande*, "race defilement," which required manpower for policing and prosecuting. Sarah Gordon and other scholars have documented hundreds of such cases. Frequently precipitated by a third party denunciation, indictments for *Rassenschande* occasionally followed an unwed couple's desire to obtain a marriage license. Those who committed *Rassenschande* tended to receive longer sentences than those who merely came to the aid of or socialized with Jews because the former was a clear violation of the law while the latter was not, per se. "Friends of Jews" were prosecuted under laws covering slander, conspiracy, and treason. Initially, sentences for *Rassenschande* involved terms in a normal prison, but by 1937, a growing number of convicts were being sent to harsher penitentiaries, and then, upon their release, to concentration camps. Cases generally dealt with Jewish men and non-Jewish women, playing again to the image of the Jewish male as a sexual predator, and sentences for Jewish men were accordingly more severe.[48]

The underground Social Democratic resistance (Sopade) listed 179 cases of *Rassenschande* from October 1935 to December 1936. Most of the sixty-eight cases reported between October 1935 and August 1936 involved Jewish men accused of having longstanding relations with Gentile women. All eight instances of *Rassenschande* in Frankfurt between 1935 and 1938, published in a compendium by historians Ernst Noam and Wolf-Arno Kropat, dealt with Jewish men and Gentile women, and the average time span of their acquaintance was five and a half years. Both Ilse A. and her brother were denounced and arrested for dating non-Jews. Ilse spent nearly nine months in jail. Although she knew that her actions were in violation of the law, she seemed positively stunned at the time: [from her testimony] "We were always with Christians..."[49] Ilse's brother was sentenced to one-and-a-half years in prison. Upon his release, the Nazis sent him to Dachau.

Documents and oral testimonies reveal, in addition, that one could commit *Rassenschande* without knowing it and that the Nazis could level charges of "racial defilement" on purely Jewish couples: Richard Limpert, the director of the Frankfurt Musicians' Orchestra, was accused of failing to sever ties with his allegedly Jewish former wife. Limpert maintained throughout the entire investigation that his wife was not Jewish. He lost his post nonetheless.[50] Gerri M., a Dutch Jew married to a German Jew, was shocked when German soldiers broke into her home (in occupied Holland) and arrested her husband on charges of "race defilement." According to Gerri, the Germans noticed that she was blonde—from head to toe, and thus regarded her as "Aryan." One of the Germans offered to help if she became his "girlfriend." She did not, and was herself deported to Westerbork and then to Bergen-Belsen.[51] For nearly a year after the war, Gerri waited for her husband to return—to no avail. However, as she embarrassingly recalls, "...in that year, I wasn't terribly faithful...In my mind, I knew that he was dead."[52]

Divorce was yet another effect of the Nuremberg Laws. By the beginning of 1939, it was clear that Jewish partners in mixed unions would lose any privileged status if their marriages were dissolved, and the pressure on non-Jewish spouses to divorce was intense, supported by the Führer himself: "Should the German wife of a Jew decide to divorce, she would be welcomed back into the German blood community and all disadvantages would be removed from her."[53] Yet most mixed marriages did not end in divorce. Ursula Büttner points out that only seven percent of such unions in Baden-Württemberg were dissolved and only ten percent in the city of Hamburg.[54] Marion Kaplan, while disputing Büttner's overly sanguine figures, also maintains that intermarriages endured:

> This was no small accomplishment, since Nazi intimidation caused grave tensions and anxieties in these marriages and the

divorce rate in the general population was on the rise. Almost immediately after 1933, intermarriages resulted in impoverishment and ostracism by former friends and colleagues. Either the 'Aryan' husband lost his position and the family had to scrape by or the 'Aryan' wife suffered the privation resulting from the radically diminished status of her Jewish husband, often losing her own job as well.[55]

In the initial phase of the "Final Solution," the Nazis made exceptions for half-Jews and some Jews living in mixed marriages (those in which the children were not raised Jewish. Mixed couples who had no children or those who raised their children as Jews were not "protected.") This special status did not necessarily guarantee exemption from discrimination, however; at Wannsee, there were proposals to sterilize Jews married to non-Jews, and many mixed children and their Jewish parents were sent to labor and concentration camps. During the infamous *Aktion Fabrik* (Factory Action) of late February 1943, intermarried Jews working in factories in Berlin were rounded up alongside other Jews to be deported.[56] Protests by church leaders and the Gentile wives of those incarcerated resulted in their eventual release. Himmler continued to reverse the trend of protecting mixed children in October 1944 by conscripting those with two Jewish grandparents into forced labor and then, in January 1945, decreeing that all Jews living in mixed marriages be sent to Theresienstadt.[57]

One of the persistent themes in testimonies of children from mixed Jewish-Christian marriages is the behavior of a non-Jewish paramour, spouse, or parent. Some remember courage, others cowardice and denunciation. Irmgard K., from Breslau, sank into a deep depression after the Nazis mandated the wearing of the yellow star in the fall of 1941. She was sustained only by the courage of her non-Jewish boyfriend:

> ...[translated from the German] 1941 came, and the war had already begun, and then there was the requirement that Jews had to wear the yellow star, and also take the names Sarah [for women] and Israel, for men. I also was made to take the name Sarah and wear the star. If I didn't have Fritz by my side, I think I would have lost the strength to go on living...I never disavowed my father...I knew I was the child with a Jewish father, but now to wear the star and take the name Sarah...that

was a horrible thing. Fritz said, when I had reached the end, 'Mädel, I'll wear the star with you, and he did….Fritz came to me only at night, because it said on the door, 'Irmgard Sarah Adam.' We couldn't see each other during the day anymore. And yet there wasn't a day that Fritz didn't come to me, even if it was only for a couple of hours…[58]

Irmgard survived Auschwitz and was able to reunite with Fritz after the war.

The motif of the "helpful Gentile mother" comes through in the following remembrances. Ernst S.'s father was incarcerated by the Nazis multiple times. But Ernst remembers the kindness of his Gentile stepmother: "My second mother stayed with us. She didn't have to do that. But she stayed with us. And her family did too. I was very touched. She didn't have to do this. She had a very difficult time." Ernst's father was one of the men given a reprieve during the *Aktion Fabrik*, but his persecution would not end there. In the winter of 1944, his father was put in jail for hiding other Jews. He was deported to Auschwitz in June.[59] For Hans L., the bravery of his non-Jewish mother sustains him as well. In 1941, Hans's mother was taken to Gestapo officials who tried to intimidate her into divorcing her Jewish husband. She refused. Hans remembers his mother relaying to him how one Gestapo official questioned her patriotism and honor. She responded, in Hans's memory, "It is exactly because I have honor I will not divorce." Hans's mother was also one of the women on the street protesting during the *Fabrik Aktion*; she was able to secure the release of her husband and son—both of whom ended up intermittently hiding and being dragooned into forced labor until the end of the war.[60]

Simply talking about marriage and intermarriage as a diversion, without real content or meaning, lifted the spirits of Israel W., incarcerated in Bunzlau. He remembers meeting a German woman working at the camp. "She said, 'my mother was Jewish. My father is SS, and he loves me. He's an engineer.'" And then, like a bolt out of the blue, this woman blurted out: "I like you…if the war would finish, would you like to marry me?" Realizing that the proposal had very little significance, Israel responded, "Why not?"[61]

For other survivors, however, memories of Jewish-Gentile relationships are punctuated by denunciation and betrayal. Kurt K. had two sisters who married non-Jews before 1933. One sister's husband disapproved of her criticism of Hitler and denounced her to the

Gestapo. "...They picked her up from the house, and sent her right away to Auschwitz...Lotte was her name." The other sister was married to a "nice," "quiet guy," in Kurt's words. "They [the Nazis?] didn't touch her."[62]   Judith B., in her testimony, demonstrates the conflation of multiple narratives (and the failure of the interviewer to sufficiently unpack them) by moving from a sentence about her family's internment in October 1938 (as Polish Jews) to a story about a classmate's mother who denounced her Jewish spouse. Apparently, the woman had the option of declaring her husband a "race-defiler" and keeping her children as "Aryan." Her husband would have been the only family member to be incarcerated. The mother signed whatever papers she needed to sign. "It sounded horrible," Judith remembers, especially when the mother tried to take her son with her. "He [Norbert] didn't want to go. He wanted to go with his father."[63]

Conclusion

The Nazi vision of a "eugenic utopia" was only partially realized. While childbirth rates increased among non-Jewish women (from 1.5 percent in 1932 to 1.9 percent in 1938), the percentage of female workers remained high (thirty-six percent, as compared to twenty six percent in England and eighteen percent in the United States).[64] Yet the Nazis were only too successful in fulfilling the exclusionary aspect of their racial program. Before the Second World War even began, they had managed to expel, persecute, violate, and in some cases, destroy, hundreds of thousands of Germans, Jews and non-Jews alike, on the basis of some predetermined "racial and genetic inferiority." In 1943, with the extermination of European Jewry well underway, Rudolf Ramm, the head of medical education in Germany, hailed the many "milestones" of the Third Reich—from the Sterilization Law to the "Blood Protection Law." Without these, he argued, Germany would not have been in the situation in which it found itself. His words were as ironic as they were prophetic.

Notes

[1] *Mein Kampf,* Trans. Ralph Manheim (Boston, 1971), 398

[2] Ibid., 401.

[3] Ibid., 403.

[4] Ibid., 404.

[5] Robert Proctor, *Racial Hygiene: Medicine under the Nazis* (Cambridge, Mass., 1988), 124

[6] The Nazi state was, as historian Robert Proctor points out, "constructed and administered almost solely by men;" of 2.5 million party members in 1935, only 5.5 percent were women, and women were barred from holding high-ranking posts in the party as early as 1921. Goebbels, as cited in "Die Stellung der Frau im Dritten Reich," *Die Gewerkschaftliche Frauenzeitung* 15 April 1931, 30. See also Proctor, 118-123.

[7] Lenz, *Archiv für Rassen- und Gesellschaftsbiologie* 10 (1913): 369, and Proctor, 123

[8] By 1938, all civil servants in Germany were required to either marry or to resign, and medical journals began publishing critiques of unmarried couples and childless marriages. After 1938, couple who had been married for five years who had not yet had a child were penalized with a tax. Proctor, 121.

[9] Proctor, 122.

[10] Ibid.

[11] In 1903, at the Ninth International Congress to Combat Alcoholism held in Bremen, Rüdin proposed sterilizing alcoholics, a suggestion that was rejected.

[12] Lenz, "Ist Sterilisierung strafbar?" *Archiv für Rassen und Gesellschaftsbiologie* 2 (1931): 232-233.

[13] Geleitwort, *Eugenik* 1 (1930): 1.

[14] Michael Burleigh, "Eugenic Utopias and the Genetic Present," *Totalitarian Movements and Political Religions* 1/1 (Summer 2000): 69.

[15] Paul Weindling, *Health, Race, and German Politics Between National Unification and Nazism* (Cambridge, 1989), 451. The 1933 Law was based on the 1932 proposal by the Prussian Health Council. Fritz Lenz believed the 1933 law was too narrow and pushed for the sterilization of one million feebleminded, one million mentally ill, and 170,000 idiots.

[16] *Mein Kampf,* 624. According to provisions of the November 1918 cease fire between the Allied Powers and Germany, Allied troops were to occupy a stretch of German territory to the west and east of the Rhine river. This occupation force (of about 100,000 soldiers) was made more permanent by the provisions of the Versailles Peace treaty, which officially marked the end of World War I. Additional Allied incursions into German territory came in 1920 (when French troops occupied Frankfurt) and in 1923, when, in response to Germany's default on reparations payments, French and Belgian troops occupied the industrial *Ruhrgebiet.* Within the French divisions were five

Moroccan regiments, fourteen Algerian and Tunisian regiments, and two Madagascar regiments. It is estimated that the number of colonial African soldiers ranged from thirty to forty thousand. Rainer Pommerin, *Sterilisierung der Rheinlandbastarde: Das Schicksal einer farbigen deutschen Minderheit, 1918-1937* (Düsseldorf, 1979), 8-10, 12.

[17] Weindling, 530.

[18] Pommerin, 78. Fischer was noted for his study of mixed children from southwest Africa—the so-called Rehoboth Bastards. These were children of Dutch men and Hottentot women, identified as "Bastaard" by Dutch authorities to identify them as hybrids, not necessarily to brand them as illegitimate (although the distinction was often blurred). In 1904, the German colonial administration controlling what is currently Namibia launched a three year war against the native Herero and Hottentot populations, who had risen up against German rule. One year after the Germans had successfully suppressed the rebellion, Fischer made an expedition to the Rehoboth colony to prove Mendelian inheritance of racial characteristics in the mixed children. Fischer published his results in 1913 as *The Rehoboth Bastards and the Bastardization Problem in Humans*. Fischer created pedigrees for twenty-three of the "Bastard" families and photographed some 300 individuals. From these, he concluded that characteristics such as eye shape, hair texture, and hair color (among others) were inherited according to Mendelian principles. Despite conceding that his subjects had many "positive traits" (like cultural "abilities"), Fischer advised colonial authorities to prevent granting them full equality:

"If these Bastards somehow are made equal with whites, Hottentot blood will enter the white race. We still do not know a great deal about the mingling of races. But we certainly do know this: Without exception, every European nation that has accepted the blood of inferior races—and only romantics can deny that Negroes, Hottentots, and many others are inferior—has paid the price for its acceptance of inferior elements with spiritual and cultural degeneration." *Die Rehobother Bastards und das Bastardierungsproblem beim Menschen. Anthropologische und ethnologische Studien am Rehobother Bastardvolk in Deutsch-südwestwafrika* (Jena, 1913), 302

(Later quote in *Eugenik* October 1930, p. 7:
...the crossing of intellectually superior races with inferiors...means a total degradation of the condition of the pure, better one...I consider this for many reasons to be correct, despite the lack of empirical proof..."

Fischer's work did not have the kind of immediate impact that one would have expected given its later notoriety. In fact, all but one of Fischer's colleagues in anthropology chose not to review the book.

The sterilization case for which Fischer was called to testify involved a seventeen year old ship steward who had been classified by the public health office in Gemersheim as being of "foreign" or "Negro" racial descent. According to the boy's mother, the father had been a colonial soldier from Madagascar; she had since remarried. On 10 June 1937, the boy was told to appear in Ludwigshafen for an investigation by professor Fischer. When the boy failed to show up, Fischer left angrily and vowed never to perform another evaluation as his time was too valuable to waste. The Gestapo subsequently found the boy aboard a Dutch ship transporting iron pyrite from Cologne to Kostheim by way of Ludwigshafen. Officials quickly seized him, charged him with engaging in treasonous activities, and dragged him off to Cologne, where his mother gave her consent for the boy to be sterilized. On June 30, the youth underwent the operation at the Protestant Hospital in Cologne.

[19] Ernst Klee, *Auschwitz, die NS-Medizin, und ihre Opfer* (Frankfurt, 1997), 438-444,

[20] Testimony of Johann H., PCN Number 632747, Survivors of the Shoah Visual History Foundation, Saarbrücken, Germany, 18 March 1998, 01:18:56.

[21] Ibid., 04:18-04:20.

[22] Ibid.

[23] Testimony of Klara N., PCN Number 627760, Survivors of the Shoah Visual History Foundation, Detmold, Germany, 10 July 1997, 02:17:40-02:23:00.

[24] The victims of sterilization were not recognized by the Federal Republic of Germany as warranting restitution until 1968. Afterwards, the government distributed to select individuals one lump sum of 5,000DM and a pension of 100DM per month; this was raised to 120 DM in 1998.
Stefan Maiwald and Gerd Mischler, *Sexualität unter dem Hakenkreuz: Manipulation und Vernichtung der Intimsphäre im NS-Staat* (Hamburg, 1999), 75-77, 82.

[25] Testimony of Klara N., Ibid., 05:28:52.

[26] Testimony of Jack O., Testimony Number 20926, Survivors of the Shoah Visual History Foundation, Dallas, United States, 11 October 1996, 02:25:10:28-03:04:20:08

[27] Ibid., 03:04:20:08-03:07:47:01

[28] Proctor, 212, 213 and his citation of the Nazi *Informationsdienst*, 20 June 1938.

[29] As cited in Hans Georg-Stümke, "From the 'People's Consciousness of Right and Wrong' to the 'Healthy Instincts of the Nation': The Persecution of Homosexuals in Nazi Germany," in Michael Burleigh, ed., *Confronting the Nazi Past: New Debates on Modern German History* (London, 1996), 160.

[30] See Rüdin's article in *Archiv für Rassen- und Gesellschaftsbiologie* 1 (1904): 99-100, and *Fortschritte der Erbpathologie* 3 (1939): 90-99.

[31] Maiwald, 188

[32] Stümke, 164.

[33] Heinz Heger, *The Men with the Pink Triangle* (London, 1980), 61.

[34] Stumke, 162.

[35] "Gads War: A Gay Holocaust Hero Will Ride," *Village Voice*, 24 June 1997, 41.

[36] Testimony of Gad B., Survivors of the Shoah Visual History Foundation, Berlin, Germany, 19 November 1996, 3:09:32-03:12:51

[37] Testimony of Stefan K., Survivors of the Shoah Visual History Foundation, PCN 25053, 14 November 1995. Under the pseudonym of Stefan K., his story appeared in German in 1991 and in English in 1995 (Litz van Dijk, *Damnded Strong Love: The True Story of Willi G. and Stefan K.* [New York, 1995]).

[38] Pre-Interview Questionnaire of Erwin W., Survivors of the Shoah Visual History Foundation, PCN 636319, and *Lamda Nachrichten*, March 1997, 17.

[39] Testimony of Peter S., Survivors of the Shoah Visual History Foundation, 11 October 1996.

[40] Maiwald, 222.

[41] Quote from Wagner: "More than 1 billion RM is spent on the genetically disabled; contrast this with the 766 million spent on the police, or the 713 million spent on local administration, and one sees what a burden and unexcelled injustice this places on the normal, healthy members of the population." Proctor 181, and his citation of "Unser Reichärtzteführer spricht," *Ziel und Weg* 5 (1933): 431-437.

[42] Andreas Rethmeier, *Nürnberger Rassengesetze und Entrechtung der Juden im Zivilrecht* (Frankfurt, 1995), 92, and his citation of the speech in the *Frankfurter Zeitung*, 14 September 1935, 3.

[43] In the beginning of their official commentary on the Nuremberg Laws, entitled, *Kommentare zur deutschen Rassengesetzgebung* (Munich, 1936), Wilhelm Stuckart and Hans Globke avoid a clear denigration of Jews by suggesting that they could be best protected by law if they were to exist separately (*Eigenleben in gesetzlichen Grenzen*), that is, apart from Germans. As for "Gypsies" and Afro-Germans, Stuckart and Globke offered the following: "According to the circular of 26 November 1935, registry officials...shall only pursue a questionable case if he suspects that one of the partners is of foreign racial stock and that German blood will be tainted (that means, for example, cases of marriage applications between Germans and 'Gypsies,' 'Negroes,' and their 'Bastards.')" *Kommentare*, 14, 195.

[44] Rethmeier, 139-141.

[45] *Statistik des deutschen Reiches: Die Bevölkerung des Deutschen Reiches nach den Ergebnissen der Volkszählung 1919: Die Juden und jüdischen Mischlinge im Deutschen Reich*, Vol. 552, Issue 4 (Berlin, 1944), 21, 32, 120-130.

[46] Michael Kater, "Everyday Antisemitism in Prewar Nazi Germany: The Popular Bases," *Yad Vashem Studies* 16 (1984).

[47] Proctor, 141, and his citation of Gütt to Himmler, 7 February 1938, Bundesarchiv, NS 19/3434.

[48] Jonathan Friedman, *The Lion and the Star: Gentile-Jewish Relations in Three Hessian Communities, 1919-1945* (Lexington, Kentucky, 1998), 149.

[49] Testimony of Ilse A., Survivors of the Shoah Visual History Foundation, n.d., n.p., 01:08:50-01:10:52.

[50] Ernst Noam and Wolf-Arno Kropat, *Juden vor Gericht, 1933-1945: Dokumente aus hessischen Justizakten mit einem Vorwort von Johannes Strelitz* (Wiesbaden, 1975), 118-169, and Richard Limpert, Akten 74/373, Stadtarchiv Frankfurt.

[51] Testimony of Gerri M., Testimony Number 6518, Survivors of the Shoah Visual History Foundation, Sydney, Australia, 27 November 1995, 02:16:28:21-02:19:37:02.

[52] Ibid., 03:20:03:22-03:23:09:03.

[53] Hitler cited by Goering in a brief in the larger report, "Questions on Jewish Policy," undertaken by the Ministry of Interior and disseminated on 12 January 1939 to all state authorities, and then by the deputy of the Führer on 17 January to all party members. See also Reithmeier, 235.

[54] Ursula Büttner, *Die Not der Juden teilen: Christlich-jüdische Familien im Dritten Reich* (Hamburg, 1988), 57, 298.

[55] Marion Kaplan, *Between Dignity and Despair: Jewish Life in Nazi Germany* (Oxford, 1998), 89.

[56] See Nathan Stolzfus, *Resistance of the Heart: Intermarriage and the Rosenstrasse Protest in Nazi Germany* (New York, 1996).

[57] Friedman, 175.

[58] Irmgard K., Main Testimony of the Survivors of the Shoah Visual History Foundation, CD-ROM, *Erinnern*, 03:09:07-03:10:33

[59] Testimony of Ernst S., Testimony Number 23340, Survivors of the Shoah Visual History Foundation, Westport, United States, 11 December 1996, 01:19:15:17-01:20:53:01.

[60] Testimony of Hans-Oskar L., PCN Number 23442, Survivors of the Shoah Visual History Foundation, Berlin, Germany, 5 March 1996, no time code.

[61] Testimony of Israel W., Testimony Number 26908, Survivors of the Shoah Visual History Foundation, Forest Hills, United States, 2 March 1997, 03:14:21:00-03:21:00:00.

[62] Testimony of Kurt K., Testimony Number 26097, Survivors of the Shoah Visual History Foundation, Philadelphia, United States, 27 February 1997, 01:17:54:06-01:23:54:01.

[63] Testimony of Judith B., Testimony Number 31699, Survivors of the Shoah Visual History Foundation, Jerusalem, Israel, 2 June 1997, 02:13:45:17-02:18:29:25.

[64] At 1.3 million, the number of births in Germany dwarfed those in England (737,000) and France (612,000). Proctor, 124, 126. See also, Tim Kirk, *The Longman Companion to Nazi* Germany (London, 1995), 73, 74.

\

Chapter 2

Gender and Nazi Exploitation

If it is contentious to approach the Third Reich as a eugenic experiment, casting it analytically as both a racist and gendered entity, it can be equally divisive, often more so, to focus on the experiences of women and the place of gender in a discussion of the Holocaust. As historians have persuasively argued, however, Jewish women bore unique burdens as both Jews and women. They were targeted differently than Jewish men. Indeed, the very separation of the sexes in the camps, men on one side, women and children on the other, was a gendered act, and race and gender underlay the premise that Jewish females were the carriers of the next generation of "vengeful Jews," a belief, icily expressed by SS chief Heinrich Himmler below, that legitimized wholesale murder:

> We came to the question: what about the women and children? I have decided to find a clear solution here too. In fact, I did not regard myself justified in exterminating the men—let us say killing them or having them killed—while letting avengers in the shape of children...grow up. The difficult decision had to be taken to make this people disappear from the face of the earth...[1]

Himmler's logic radically altered the historical disposition of women vis-à-vis conquering armies during World War II. As Joan Ringelheim points out, while the Nazis intended to kill every single man, woman, and child they could define as Jewish, "the Final Solution

was…one of the first such events in history that did not treat the female
population primarily as spoils of war but instead explicitly sentenced
women and children to death."[2] In addition, Ringelheim emphasizes
the disparity in chances for survival between Jewish women and men:

> My work on deportation and death figures connected with the
> mobile killing operations, ghettos, and camps has led me to
> conclude that more Jewish women were deported than Jewish
> men and that more Jewish women were killed than Jewish men.
> Jewish women's chances for survival were not equivalent to
> those of Jewish men…Women were considered less valuable
> than men as workers, more dangerous as mothers and hence
> women were immediately expendable. If it cannot be
> questioned that being Jewish mattered during the Holocaust,
> then it does not seem possible to question that being male or
> female also mattered. The essential question is how being male
> or female made a difference, not whether it did.[3]

Women also endured experiences that men could not by virtue
of simple biology, birthing and menstruation chief among them. These
uniquely female life cycles added layers of fragility to the experience of
Jewish women because they were often accompanied by sexual abuse,
emotional and physical pain, and the threat of death for both mother
and child.   Marlene Heinemann reminds us that "women whose
pregnancy showed up after admission to the camps were usually put to
death, or labor was induced early and the infant killed…Some
expectant mothers at Auschwitz were able to save their own lives by
having secret abortions with the help of some inmate physicians or
killing their babies…"[4]
This is not to suggest that men did not have equally unique
experiences because of their sex. Quite the contrary, Jewish men,
marked by circumcision, were confronted by their sexual difference on
a daily basis, often resorting to self-mutilation to conceal their indelible
feature. Jewish men somehow stood for a "lower," "weakened," and
"feminized" form of sexuality within Nazism as they were seen as no
less genitally "different" from non-Jewish men than women:

> Just as Nazi atrocity attacked Jewish women both as Jews and as
> women, it also attacked Jewish men both as Jews and as men.
> Often, Nazi brutality took the form of attacks on male biology,
> on the secondary sex characteristics that made Jewish men

publicly recognizable as Jewish men: bears and earlocks. Like women, men were forced to endure the public exposure and shaving of their genital hair. Circumcision made Jewish men easily identifiable and, hence, particularly vulnerable.[5]

Pregnancy and Birth

In this survey, survivors who became pregnant during the "Final Solution," or who had some experience with pregnancy, came from a wide range of backgrounds and nationalities and most were teenagers when the war began. Many of their testimonies are fragmentary and serve, at best, as confirmation of various themes. One of these constants is the tangible threat pregnancy posed to the lives of the mother and infant, both in terms of the physical risks of delivery and the danger of being discovered by the Nazis or denounced by friends and allies.

Fleeting discussions of pregnancy and abortion in the concentration and extermination camps are especially abundant. At Auschwitz, Toby K. took newborns, wrapped them in blankets, and put them in a pile outside the barracks to die "because women weren't allowed to keep let alone feed the babies, even if they could..."[6] Magda S., while interned in the Kophaza camp in Hungary, was forced to aid a doctor perform an abortion on a woman who had been impregnated by an SS soldier. "They made an abortion, and I had to be there. It was the first time I even heard about abortion."[7] Martha V. became pregnant in the Sered camp in Czechoslovakia and was told by a doctor that if she were taken to Auschwitz, she and the baby would be killed. Consequently, she underwent an abortion-- "without any medication...any, not really in a medical surroundings, but they said, just to survive, I should go through with it."[8] While in an Italian camp in Yugoslavia, Jean S. witnessed a birth: "[It was] right there on the floor. The baby stayed with her. The woman was very healthy. [There was] no such horror like in [the] German camps..."[9] For her part, Mary W. met her husband Fritz while interned in the Rab Island camp also in Yugoslavia. After Italy capitulated in September 1943, the prisoners of Rab were released, and Mary and Fritz fled to the mountains. Mary became pregnant, but lost her husband to pneumonia in March 1944. "I had the option for an abortion...but, that's all I have left...The day before I gave birth, I didn't even have a diaper." Mary gave birth in November, but her baby died of starvation two months later.[10]   In a small but no less moving fragment of memory, Eva S. remembers a cousin who gave birth in Bergen Belsen. "She would wash the baby with her own spit."[11]

Testimonies dealing with ghetto life are similarly replete with vignettes of pregnancy, and the threats to women's lives that operated in the camps were present in the ghettos as well. According to Ruth Schwertfeger, for instance, Nazi officials in Theresienstadt mandated abortions for pregnant women.[12]   In the Warsaw ghetto, Irena S. went to a doctor friend who performed a hazardous abortion on her in his basement. Later the same day, she managed to escape from a round-up of Jews.[13]   Emil N. remembers: "I was with my wife after this so-called ceremony [in the Starachowice ghetto]. She got pregnant. We didn't know what we were doing. The blood of youngsters is different. I said that she should go to do something by a doctor. She didn't know what to do...She said she was afraid." [14] Rena G. insists that her "most difficult memory" of the Radom ghetto was the termination of her pregnancy.[15]   Finally, Rachel D., recalls that she and her husband were together for six weeks in the Vilna ghetto when she became pregnant and was faced with the decision to abort.   Her dilemma was compounded by her mother who believed that if she [Rachel] were to undergo an abortion, she would never be able to conceive.

Survivor sketches of childbirth often convey and confirm multiple pieces of information.   For instance, Germaine P. discusses encounters she had with pregnant women in Auschwitz alongside commentary over the issue of amenorrhea in the camp and the sterilization procedure she endured: "One day, the Nazis came and asked who was pregnant. [They] said that they would take care of them, and give them food...they took them to the gas chamber..." As for her operation, she tells of having a fever and severe vomiting afterwards, and in one unverifiable memory, she tells of a female prisoner who had electrodes inserted into her uterus to destroy her ovaries. She also links a time when she was forced to pick flowers with the loss of her menstrual cycle: "Why they wanted to use these flowers?" she asked the camp guard. He said, "they give it to people to destroy the period..."[16]

There are also fragments that are corroborated independently by other testimonies. The account from Janos S., is one of the few male testimonies to speak to the issue of pregnancy. It is also unique in that it does not involve the death of either the mother or the baby; one should not infer from this a particular gender slant—only that this was an isolated incident. "One woman towards the end gave birth...the commandant (of Mühldorf) knew and hid the child. I guess he knew the end was coming, so he tried to do some good..."[17] Corroborative testimony comes from Helene U., who was also in Mühldorf but appears to have no connection to Janos S. Helene remembers a woman in an implausibly similar circumstance who was able to keep her baby close to the time of the camp's liberation. "I week later, another woman had a girl, but the SS officials determined that the baby should live, perhaps to appease [the] Americans?"[18]

Several images recur in testimonies about pregnancy and abortion. Among this intermittent imagery is that of a garbage pail. Linda M., from Skarszysko-Kamienna: "One of the girls had a baby. She was married and separated from her husband. After she had the baby, she threw it in the garbage pail and covered it up...She knew if she [had been] caught, she'd be killed...The Nazis threw it out..."[19] Fanny L, also from Auschwitz, remembers a pregnant girl from the same city as her cousin. "She was an untouchable...Hungarian soldiers had raped her..." Fanny's cousin delivered the baby. "...a big baby, but stillborn..." Fanny took the baby in a pail to the bathroom and buried in the excrement.[20]

Some of the fragments from testimony merely intimate the fate of pregnant women or base their telling on hearsay and rumor. While this is indeed problematic, it does not render these memories "invalid" or somehow less "useful." Other themes may emerge from the recollection, themes such as disbelief. Herta M.'s memory of her imprisonment in Auschwitz typifies this bewilderment: "We did not know what they were doing there...We were cold...and we were in Birkenau. Everything was wet, muddy...[In the] barracks, [there were] eight people per platform...[We] later found out that some of the girls were pregnant. Many had miscarriages or buried their babies. Still, we didn't know why [we] were there or what they were doing?"[21]

These fragments offer insight into the psychology and mental state of the survivor as well. Eva S.'s cousin Lilly became pregnant at Auschwitz. (In her testimony, when she comes to this story, she drops all eye contact with the camera and begins to cry). "[Lilly] was in the ninth month, but they didn't notice, and she wasn't sent to the gas chamber. She was very tiny and just looked fat...The Block Elder suffocated the baby..."[22] From Shary N.: "There was a girl who was pregnant, three months...[she] was able to hide, but when she began to show...the doctor found out...She gave birth to a boy. The doctor took

it. One day later, he came back and said the baby was dead." The
doctor allowed the woman to bury her baby with fifty of her female
workmates. "And I don't think I ever cried as much as I cried then.
We said Kaddish for that baby. That was the worst thing that I
experienced there. The very worst..."²³   Magdalena V. worked in the
camp hospital at Auschwitz, where she had one experience with a
pregnant woman who gave birth. "One night, a woman went into labor.
The Nazis took her to hospital. They put her on a cement slab. [I] saw
this...[I] wanted to go to her. This woman gave birth by herself, no
doctor, no nurse. She was in intense pain. The soldier came in and
wrapped the child away in a blanket and then [I] was told to take it
from them...The baby was dead...This was such a terrible
experience...I was sixteen years old...Later on, I found out that they
just put the baby on a fire. I never saw the mother again...[I] said right
then, 'I don't want to have a baby ever... '"²⁴

Recollections of pregnancy and birth, whether eyewitness or
second-hand, demonstrate the importance of context and milieu.
Survivors who describe pregnancies in either the ghettos or in hiding do
not uniformly end in the death of babies or mothers, unlike the vast
majority of testimonies of births in the camps. Moreover, many of the
women who tell of experiences in the ghettos or in hiding were the ones
who were actually pregnant, while camp survivors convey their
memories essentially as eyewitnesses or participants in infanticides and
abortions. The language in all is equally scarred and painful. In some
instances, language and story become stripped to their bare minimum
and often break down completely when the survivor becomes, once
again, the mother who lost a child.

From Nellie A., who gave birth in the Lodz ghetto, Chasia K.,
who was pregnant in the Kovno ghetto, and Luba L., who had a child in
Warsaw, we have some very vivid reminiscences:

> [from Nellie A.]....I was married and got pregnant. When I
> started to show, [the people hiding me] made a grave for me in a
> cellar. I felt like screaming. I would put my hand over my
> mouth. It was dark, cold. It was like being buried alive, being
> in a grave and not being able to come out. After a while, I
> started to think about the baby, the life in me, and that was
> something incredible. That occupied my time. When I had
> dreams, I would dream about my mother, who would talk to me
> gently and say in won't be over long, have patience. I would
> feel much better. She would be the one to carry me through the

month and months when it wasn't night and it wasn't day...A woman came down with a little kerosene lamp and helped me bring the baby into the world. He was beautiful. I was able to nurse him. I stayed there until my liberation by the Russians.[25]

[from Chasia K]...When I gave birth,...[there was] no sanitation. [We] did have a stove that warmed the room. It gave off so much smoke...The baby was born in this small room. My mother and a nurse were there when I gave birth. I was suffering very much, but I gave birth. The baby's name was Tikvah, [meaning] hope--hope that she would bring a better future. I didn't have anything to wrap it. I used the cover of a piano. My mother tore it into pieces to wrap her in it. I gave her to eat scraps, no breast milk. My mother cooked kasha. My doctor said that it was unbelievable that her intestines could take it. Impossible. But she did. She grew and was developed and was talking and knew what was clever...She knew Germans. She knew [when to] hide.[26]
(Chasia's child was killed in 1944 during an *Aktion* to clear the Kovno ghetto).

[from Luba L.--note the similar passages and the similarity in language]...I was pregnant. I didn't want to die. But I bought a piece of poison with bread. If the Nazis were close to killing me, I would kill myself...I had the baby in a bathroom in 1941 in April. I named her Zelda, but I called her Zenia. There was a lady, a midwife, who put a handkerchief in my mouth. I wanted to scream. I was in labor from Friday to Monday. The woman said only bite. [Zelda] was a scrawny little girl. I thought [she] would die of starvation. She didn't. She grew up...She didn't cry at night. I was in such pain in the morning, but the baby didn't cry...She was four years old when they killed her...[27]
(After escaping to Czestochowa, Luba was caught by the Nazis and placed in a forced labor camp. She hid Zelda with other children in a bunker under her barracks. Six months before liberation, the children were discovered and executed.)

What is striking in each of these excerpts is the close pairing of desperate and joyful imagery and the choice, conscious or not, to employ simple sentence structure when describing the infants. Thus, Nellie's boy was "beautiful;" Chasia's girl was "hope;" Luba's girl "grew up." Only one second-hand account of a ghetto birth that I surveyed, that of a man--Benesch T., was even remotely parallel in description. Benesch's wife, like Chasia K., had a child in Kovno:

> ...She gave birth under completely abnormal conditions. The child was born on March 4, 1941. Her name was Aviva. We gave her that name because we couldn't find a better name, and it was spring. Aviva means daughter of spring. I didn't have the means to raise the baby. [We didn't have] a crib. I put two chairs together and a board on the side of the chairs. That was the crib. My wife gave birth in the home. The doctor that came was a friend of ours. My wife nursed but didn't have enough milk because she didn't have enough to eat. I gave her whatever I could. Luckily, the baby was a healthy one...[28]
> (Benesch was able to hide Aviva with a Christian woman. He and his wife were reunited with Aviva after the war.)

Lennie J. became pregnant while hiding in the Netherlands in 1943:

> My husband was religious, and we didn't know how long the war would last. So something happened. Very foolish. I had a hard time with the child. Bombs were dropping. We didn't get enough to eat. People from the underground brought us some coupons so that we could eat...[We] stayed in a ten foot by twelve foot room, just a bed and wash basin. I had a table. My husband took care so that there were some books...It was not an easy pregnancy. When the baby was due, I was in terrible pain. I had to put a pillow over my head. For four days, I was in labor. The lady who was hiding us didn't want to go to the doctor. But I was almost dying and the baby, too. My husband said [to the woman], 'I'm going to go, and if they catch me, they'll catch you too.' So she finally went to [the] doctor. The doctor delivered it. [He] put the baby in a paper carton with a pillow. The man from the underground took him away from me...I got very sick, with a 104, 105 degree fever...I said, 'Just tell me he is safe.' They did and I thought now I can die..."
> (Lennie named the boy Herstring—for autumn because he was born on September 21. She and her baby would be helped by different underground fighters until the end of the war, when the two were finally reunited.)[29]

The testimony of Bronka K., who also went into hiding, is a more devastating example of a survivor coping with multiple traumas.

After learning that she was to be sent to a concentration camp, Bronka fled and met members of the Soviet resistance. While a part of the underground, she remembers assisting a woman who gave birth. "She bit my hands. Without a word, she had the baby...I wouldn't let her see the baby. The man that stood by with me in the bunker helped. [He] took a piece of wood and smashed the baby, when he started to cry, he strangled it and wrapped it in a sack of potatoes. Several days later, there was a terrible smell. The placenta came out. [I] had to cut it. The mother got fever. Another thing came out, a black substance that smelled. That was the placenta..."[30]

Bronka herself became pregnant while in hiding. She was liberated and went to the Soviet Union before she gave birth. "I walked in the middle of the night...in such pain...I fell on train tracks...[but I] reached the hospital and had a girl, Tamara. She died two months later. I don't know how I feel. So devastated. [I] buried her on January 20, 1945...I had no milk to give her." It is at this point that Bronka's testimony falls apart temporally. She states that she turned to prostitution (but does not say when, either before her child's conception or after her death). "I was a prostitute, so disgusting, ugly...Luckily, nobody came over to me...But then I came back to normal...I got pregnant from a man who helped me. My children wanted to know the truth about me. I never talked about it. I always felt guilty. Why? It wasn't my doing. It was forced on me..."

Bronka then goes on to say that she had been repeatedly raped while in hiding and during liberation. According to her testimony, she was raped by a resistance fighter: "He needed sex...there was nothing I could do...that went on for a few weeks. I had no feelings left..." And then she was raped by a Pole after liberation: "I put lipstick on...We were waving to soldiers, flirting with them. Then [we] went to the forests, fields and came to a town where we knew a woman who had a bunker. Polish men [approached us.] All of a sudden, every one of them needs sex. What the hell is it with men? With guns over our head, we allowed them to screw our legs. Fine. Fine. Go to hell. But they didn't kill us."[31]

After the war, Bronka went to Paris where she met her future husband. The two went to Canada in the fifties. She now has three children. She claims she has had a "funny life, a beautiful life...I used to feel ashamed, guilty. I still fantasize that one day someone would come around and say that my sister is alive. Or that my father's been found. I live in a world of let's pretend...Look where it got me..."[32]

Menstruation

Many, if not most women lost their periods in the concentration camps. The exact cause (or causes) of amenorrhea, however, is the subject of wild speculation. Some survivors believe that the Nazis deliberately placed a poisonous agent or drug in their soup, while others point to starvation and the overall trauma of being incarcerated in a camp. Yet women's menstrual cycles were disrupted in settings other than the camps, in ghettos and hiding places, making the occurrence of the event more salient than the origins by virtue of its commonality and impact on the psyche of thousands of women. As Marleine Heineman notes, "Amenorrhea must be considered a form of psychological assault on a woman's identity, since most women had no idea whether fertility would return if they survived..."[33]

Survivors who attest that a specific agent disrupted their menstrual cycles are almost universally survivors of a camp experience. Sabina M. also remembers getting a shot at the Bendorf concentration camp. In her recollection, she received one shot, in the belly. She didn't menstruate again until after the war. "Some people, never came back their menstruation."[34]   Sarah W. claims that she had to stand in line "for needles...We didn't know what they were for. I think later on, that was to stop our periods..."[35] Before the war, Eva S. had begun menstruating, but she stopped after she came to Auschwitz: "That was the terrible thing, they gave us something in the soup to stop menstruation for sanitary reasons."[36]   One of the older survivors in this survey, Doba A. was in her late twenties when she was sent to Majdanek.   "That was the last time, [they] got their periods until liberation...Either they put something in the food, I don't know what it was..."[37]   Luba S., interned in Ravensbrück, makes a similar contention: "They put powder in the food....But it wasn't a secret...to prevent menstruation." After the war, she went to a doctor because her cycle had not returned. Three months after this visit, it did.[38]   Golda N., in her mid twenties when she was interned in Leipzig-Schönefeld, likewise insists that the Nazis put something in their food. It was not until she was fed a different meal that she was able to menstruate again. "...from the herring! A nice huge piece, salted...it opened up my canals!" [to the cameraman] Excuse me my dear boy."[39] Phyllis P., an Auschwitz survivor, suggests a different agent: "...[They gave us] coffee that was like washwater." It was this "coffee," Phyllis maintains, that caused her to lose her period.[40]

Only a few testimonies surveyed placed blame for amenorrhea on something less intentional, such as for instance, a lack of food. Joan W. is one of the few to claim that she stopped menstruating because of malnutrition. "[We] five girls watched out for each other. We ate out of one bowl with five spoons. We ate in a bowl in which we made at night..."[41] Rachela P.'s interviewer also questions the "poisonous agent" theory. Rachel was imprisoned in Ravensbrück: "Later we found out that they gave us something in the soup to stop menstruating." [Interviewer]: "I think it would have stopped anyway." Rachel: "I don't know. As soon as we came to Majdanek we did not menstruate at all."[42]

Fewer women still discuss amenorrhea in the context of the ghetto. What is said, however, suggests that hunger, disease, and starvation, rather than poison or other Nazi devices, caused the loss of menstruation. Greta K., among others, asserts "I didn't menstruate [in the Lodz ghetto]. There was no food. I thought I'd never have one. But after the war, six months, I got it..."[43] Dresla S., also in Lodz, avers exactly the same thing.[44] Only Bianka K., from Warsaw, describes how she *began* menstruating in the ghetto, but she is younger than either Dresla and Greta, by thirteen and five years respectively, and was probably in better physical health when she experienced her first period in the ghetto.[45]

The occasional reference to menstruation from survivors who hid lends credibility to the association of amenorrhea with hunger. Bebe F. was able to find a hiding place with her family near Antwerp. She would spend her time cutting out pictures of American movie stars from magazines she found. "...I wanted to grow up like Alice Faye..." She was nearly thirteen when she went into hiding. "I still played with dolls and then I had to grow up fast..." In the attic of the house that served as her hiding place, Bebe had her first period. "I didn't know...my parents didn't discuss..." Bebe remembers that her mother stopped menstruating and initially thought she was pregnant; she wasn't—it was menopause. Bebe insists that it was brought on by malnutrition.[46] Hanka C., hiding in Poland, puts it simply:" "I lost my period. There was no water, no food."[47]

Humiliation

The Nazis dehumanized their victims in a variety of ways in the camps; one of the methods that stripped individuals of their dignity and sexuality almost immediately was the shearing of hair. Describing her arrival at Auschwitz, Ibolya S remembers: "They shaved us. Every single hair in your body...was gone...We didn't recognize each other. You have this hair...You didn't recognize yourself."[48] Herta M., also at Auschwitz: "They cut our hair all over...I looked and there was a window and I had no hair. They didn't shave it straight, like steps."[49] Abraham B., a prisoner at the Treblinka extermination camp, worked in the gas chambers where he cut the hair of women who were to be executed. "I was a barber. Not a bad one. They assigned me to cut off the hair of women before they were gassed...Women were sitting naked on the benches. We had to cut off hair and make believe that they were going to take a shower. They gave us scissors to cut [their] hair. When we were finished, they told us to step outside, and they were gassed. After we were finished with one transport, one came in again. I had a conversation with a girl. I never knew the girl. The most gorgeous girl I knew. She said, 'Listen, you are a young man. Try to escape from here and let the world know what was going on.'" Abraham escaped from Treblinka in 1943 and made his way back to Czestochowa.[50]

SS guards subjected women to further humiliations in the latrines and showers. According to historian Vera Laska:

> On the rare occasions that the women were marched to the real showers...the grapevine somehow always reached the lewdest of the SS, who came to jeer, tease, and taunt the defenseless women. Stripping the women naked was also practiced at times of camp selections, or on long and boring Sunday afternoons, when the SS had nothing better to do than to order a roll call and expose the powerless women to a cruel parade...The depravity of the men, indulging themselves in this cheapest, basest and most disgusting of games, as much for the pleasure of seeing naked females as for the sport of frightening them out of their minds, was one of the cruelest tortures to which women were subjected in the concentration camps...Those newly arrived to these jaws of hell were crushed under the deluge of foul language, obscene gestures and the fact that they were paraded

like cattle on the market in front of men. To many women it meant an unforgivable and never to be forgotten humiliation.[51]

Rachel D., remembers the mere disgust at having to undress for an inspection at the Riga-Strasdenhof camp. "The doctor came in and said you have to undress completely naked...There were beautiful girls, young children that weren't even married, standing to get checked for lice. I just felt sorry for the girls. When I married, it came with love, but these girls (who went to the SS to have sex), we know what they had to do. It was a shame even to talk about it."[52]

A point of degradation for Jewish men often took the form of self-concealment and disfigurement, as many attempted to "alter" their circumcised penises in the hopes of passing as Gentile. Alex C. spent the entire war staying ahead of his captors, whether they were in Poland, Czechoslovakia, Hungary, or Rumania. He possessed forged papers that allowed him to move around with relative ease, and he lived day to day as a hustler on the black market. But he knew, or at least felt, that he still bore the ineffaceable mark that branded him as a Jew—his genitalia. He therefore found a surgeon in his underground world who agreed to perform the excruciating operation—aware all the while of operations which failed and resulted either in deforming scars or fatal infections. Alex's procedure was not in and of itself a success: the operation left a noticeable scar, and he still had to resort to a bribe when Rumanian doctors who figured him as a Jew were not swayed by what they saw.[53] William D. passed as a Polish Gentile to be able to work in Germany in 1942. During a random inspection for venereal disease at his job, however, his ruse was nearly discovered. "I had to undress to full nudity, put our dress in front of us, and the doctor will inspect us for venereal diseases...so for me it was not simple...being Jewish from my birth and being circumcised." William stood in a row as a German officer began conducting the examinations. He remembers that the soldier wore white leather gloves, had a shaved head, and sported a moustache. When he stopped in front of William, he remarked, "what is this one doing here? He's a cossack!" to which William abruptly responded, in German, "*Ein Cossack von Warschau!* (A cossack from Warsaw!)" The soldier apparently smiled and walked on.[54]

Sexual assault and rape

Marlene Heinemann asserts that "...rape did occur in ghettos and even some camps despite subsequent punishment..." but she qualifies her statement by saying that "the most universal form of sexual assault on women appears to have been verbal abuse..."[55] What I have found favors a more extensive view of sexual assault: Shoah Foundation testimonies of women who were victims of specific acts of sexual abuse are numerous and geographically diverse. Some of the survivors are from Poland, some are from Czechoslovakia, some from Belarus, some from Germany, and some from Hungary. Moreover, incidents of sexual assault and rape occurred in diverse settings—in the ghettos, in camps, and in hiding places. From the perspective of language, the same tropological use of contrast (beauty paired with violation, courage paired with shame) that was evident in descriptions of childbirth operated in recollections of sexual abuse.

The one unifying factor in these testimonies is gender— women violated by men, by Germans, Poles, Czechs, Russians, Hungarians, on down the list, even, as difficult as it is to confront and admit, by some Jewish men. But even here, the generalization breaks down. I found several testimonies of men detailing sexual abuse, suggesting that many more might be found in the thousands of tapes that remain to be catalogued at the Foundation. Men were clearly not alone as victims of sexual assault, contrary to Marlene Heinemann's contention:

> ...While the exchange of sex for greater survival odds may at times be a part of the male prisoners' experience, it occurs only in more restricted form in the male-written literature surveyed. Usually it is voluntary and involves a homosexual relationship between a younger person, 'the pipel,' and a kapo, i.e., a prisoner functionary...The exploitation of sexual abuse by SS officials as an instrument of terror and control occurs primarily between SS officials, either male or female, and the female inmates...Male prisoners...do not portray themselves as being subjected to sexual assault by the SS or punished for refusing prostitution...[56]

Ghetto Accounts

Inge F. , interned in Theresienstadt, describes the lasting impact of being raped by a German officer:

I was very hungry. Somebody in Terezin gave me a piece of bread and a German saw it. He took me and raped me and said if I wanted the bread I had to earn it. I didn't eat it. I didn't want it anymore. Then I started to grow up and see. I am nothing. They can do whatever they want. I never told anyone. I don't want my brother to know. I am so very ashamed. I am seventy and still ashamed. It shouldn't have happened that way...I never married. I used to like men. Now I tolerate them. I couldn't stand the thought of going to bed with them...[57]

Bina W., from Lodz, remembers that she had to appear before Hans Biebow, the Nazi administrator of the ghetto: "I am ashamed to tell you. Hans Biebow came once at night and picked me out to undress naked..."[58] Mina L., tells of a German soldier who tried to rape her and her sisters one night in the Nowa Wies ghetto: "My sister jumped out of bed. We saw he was completely drunk. He was outraged, mad. He went to the door and ripped off the mezuzah. Then my sister talked to him. He calmed down and even apologized. It was a miracle. In that half-hour, we were terrified. He left after two hours. He didn't touch us."[59]

Dana S., from Lvov, speaks in allusions and appears desperate to affix a positive ending to her violation:

...I was playing with friends...A German soldier came over, tall, with a part in his hair, and he had a case of papers. He took me by the hand. I was scared. He squatted down and started to grope me under my dress. He took out a tomato and said, bite it. I knew that no possible good could come of this because I knew about 'Snow White' and the apple. And he was just as wicked. He showed me his gun. I remembered, would I be shot if I ran to [my] apartment which I could see. I ran, but he didn't shoot...my mother made a bath and hugged me and put me to bed. She didn't ask any questions. I felt really grateful and it was OK...[60]

Accounts from men and women who witnessed rapes and coerced sex are no less disturbing, implicating Germans and a wide array of allies and collaborators. Bernard Z., in the Tacovo ghetto, in Czechoslovakia, recalls: "The [Hungarian] guards would take out young girls and do whatever they wanted to do with them. The girls would come back crying. The mothers would be beaten for trying to protect them."[61]   From Imre H., in the Satoraljaujhely ghetto in Hungary:

> ...A young lady, about 17, was the most beautiful thing I'd ever seen in my life. A drunk Hungarian gendarme told her to take off her clothes. He approached her and ripped off her blouse. She was standing there. He wanted to rape her. He asked his comrades to help. They raped her in the synagogue. It was the first time I ever saw a naked lady.[62]

> From Malka W.:
> I remember there was a rape from the police. In the next room in our home there was a family. They had a beautiful girl, Peshke. I remember this. A [German] policeman got drunk, and he came to have a good time. He sent everybody out and remained with Peshke. My father was very brave. He ran into the room, and I ran in behind him. I took his rifle from the room. My father and my brothers threw him and the rifle out...[63]

> From Paula H. in Prszemysl:
> ...[the Gestapo head] Reisener [sic]...found my niece, [my] husband's brother's daughter. She looked like a young Elizabeth Taylor. He took her out of the ghetto. He loved her. We thought he was going to kill her. He was a good-looking man. During [the] second *Aktion*, he knew he wasn't allowed to live with a Jewish girl. He knew she was going to be killed. He took her to the train. He killed her before she would go to Auschwitz...[64]

Prostitution was also a fact of life in the ghetto, for, according to Charles Roland, "as long as men were willing and able to pay, the trade offered a means of earning bread, and perhaps feeding a family."[65]   Thus we find Chaim Rumkowski, head of the Lodz ghetto, in one of his earliest communications with Nazi authorities, pressing for a hospital with wards for surgery, internal medicine, pediatrics,

expectant mothers, and a special division for prostitutes.[66]   In the
Shanghai ghetto, Sigmund T. remembers as a child that "there were
refugee women working in bordellos. My father knew a man who had
been a peddler. They were visiting [this man, his daughter, and
grandson—not the husband]...I saw a Japanese official drive up, and
the daughter went off with [him]." Sigmund's parents quickly grabbed
him as he played with the peddler's grandson. The boy told Sigmund,
"My mother has lots of friends..." Sigmund also recalls a barmaid who
lived in his building who also traded sex for money and food.[67]

        In what can only be described as the darker and certainly more
controversial side of Jewish life in the ghetto, Rita H., from Pabianice
in Poland, and Gina L. from Lodz, insist that sexual crimes were
committed by Jewish community leaders.   Rita remembers that,
"Judenrat leader Rubinstein owned a grocery store before the war. I
knew his wife and knew his son. He started molesting me when I came
for milk for my mother. My friends [would say] that this is the only
way to get favors from him."[68]   Gina L. takes on an even larger and
more well-known figure: "I was afraid of Rumkowski. When he liked
a young girl, he wanted to sleep with her. [The] husband [of a friend of
mine] was a judge before the war. Rumkowski wanted to sleep with
her, so he had her husband [Molek B.] deported. She was a very, very
good friend. Any time Rumkowski came, I was going right away to the
bathroom to hide."[69] As a second-hand account, Gina's testimony is
dubious, and it is sometimes impossible to follow her narrative let
alone corroborate her accusation.[70]   From a linguistic standpoint,
however, it is quite revealing; it captures Gina's hatred of Rumkowski
in perhaps the only words and images available to her, even if these
words and images are misleading.

Camp Accounts

        Ironically, in the sample of testimonies I viewed that relate
stories of rape in the camps, I have fewer first hand accounts from
women. That does not mean, of course, that witnesses outnumbered
actual victims (and I do consider liaisons between female prisoners and
guards in the next chapter). It is more likely that once the Shoah
Foundation catalogues more testimonies, more victim accounts will
emerge. The problem with many of the second hand recollections,
however, is that they seem to be based less on an actual events than on

rumors and innuendoes. Shary N., remembers a girl from Nyirbator who was in the same barracks as she in Auschwitz. "The Germans didn't cut her hair. This girl was sent to the German barracks. After a week, the girl went crazy and ran into the electric wire. They used them [sic?] every night sexually."[71]

From Deborah S., we have the following second hand account: "One of our Dutch women, a big woman, went one night to the bathroom. You had to go quite frequently—you had the runs. She was raped by one of the guards. The next morning, she was pulled out of the barrack and taken to the gas chamber…" When asked by her interviewer how she knew the fate of the woman, however, Deborah admits that she heard it as a rumor through the "grapevine." [72]   Bronia S., heard of rapes from an ethnic German who worked with her at the factory near the Skarszysko-Kamienna camp in Poland. "The Germans would take girls, rape then, and then kill them. They shot them. They were ashamed…They wanted after they raped them, they wanted to wipe up the evidence."[73]

According to Vera Laska, "occasional prostitution, paid in goods or favors, also existed among inmates of the opposite sex. In some concentration camps, the SS had brothels available, as did a few selected privileged inmates. Most of all, however, the SS guards had a better selection of sexual partners among their own kind."[74]   This latter contention is supported by Olga Lengyel, a survivor of Auschwitz, who maintains that the SS was supplied with brothels so that they "might not become overly excited by the presence of many young and beautiful internees whom they saw naked and in every degree of exposure."[75]   Unfortunately, tales of prostitution in the camps and forced relationships between SS officials and women are frequently unsubstantiated in the Shoah Foundation's testimonies. Coenraad R., for instance, insists that women were forced to have sex with guards at Flossenbürg, but he offers little more than conjecture. "The camp commandant didn't like that the dead were slid into the crematorium because this happened to be next to the 'puff'…That was a room in the barracks where women gave sexual favors to guards or prominents. The women had to do that. [It] was the only way to stay alive."[76]

There is one especially gruesome account of sexual abuse of women from a male prisoner, Hermann S., who witnessed an atrocity while working at one of the crematoria at Auschwitz:

[There was] a woman, thirty-two or thirty-five, blond hair, blue eyes, naked...Mengele was...yelling at her, 'Are you Jewish? Are you Jewish?' She said, 'Yes.' Mengele took his cane and wrapped it around her neck. She pushed Mengele [and] knocked him back. The SS men pushed her down and when she was down, Mengele took his cane and sodomized her with it...I saw the blood coming out just like a river. He let her lying like that for two hours. And she was bleeding to death. He pulls out the cane, puts it against the wall. He told me to put her in the crematorium...I put her in a wheelbarrow. She was still faintly alive. I started saying the prayer for the dead and wheeled her around to the door...I didn't see anything, didn't know nothing. What can I do? I couldn't help her. I couldn't do nothing. I was just like a newborn child comes out, you know, in a few minutes...is helpless."[77]

Like so many other testimonies scarred by such trauma, Hermann's account falls apart towards the end of his narration when the magnitude of the event he witnessed and the extraordinary level of guilt that lingers within him begin to defy explication. The day after the brutal murder, Hermann was instructed to remove the "paint," i.e., the blood, on the cane. He shaved it off, sanded away the remainder, and was told never to return to the crematorium.[78]

As mentioned above, there are accounts of sexual abuse suffered by men in the camps. Imprisoned at the Magdeburg camp in Germany, Harry B. remembered a Hungarian Jew whose son was abused by camp officials. "[In the] morning, [they] brought him back...the kid was crying and the father was crying along with him. He wanted to go in his place. The German forced the son to be his father's hangman, to kick the box out from under him when his father was being executed. His father was begging him to kick it. He wouldn't. The German slapped him and he eventually kicked the box."[79] Nathan O. endured physical beatings and sexual assault at Gusen. One of the Block elders took him to one of the bathrooms and sodomized him. The desperation in Nathan's words at this point in his testimony is palpable. "I don't know...I managed...or what. I washed myself up...went to work. People were freezing to death. I don't know. A lot of people were reporting to the sick bed...who cared?"[80]

Interned in Warsaw, Eugene L., an Orthodox Jew, remembers a German Block Elder who made him a messenger in return for sex. His testimony is punctured by frequent paroxysms of uncontrolled crying, as he is clearly unable to reconcile his religious beliefs with the violation he suffered. "All night, he wants me to come to his room...He wants to kiss me...He started fondling me, touching me. He wanted to penetrate me..." (At this point in the story, Eugene is almost inconsolable.) The theme of sexual harassment emerges again at a later point in his story. While at the Kaufering camp in Germany, he passed out after a strenuous day of work. When he came to, he remembers a Camp Elder smiling and saying, "I've finally got you where I want you." Eugene tried to plea in German, but it is unclear what happens next. Unlike his earlier description, in this later event, Eugene only implies molestation, but the trauma is no less evident. "I didn't know what happened. I really...maybe because this went on for hours...I got dressed and went back to the barracks."[81]

Some first-hand accounts of rape and sexual abuse of men raise more questions than they answer. According to Douglas F., for instance, a Polish kapo "attempted" to rape him in Auschwitz. But his testimony suggests that the kapo actually *did* rape him. "He was tall, good looking. He shoved me into the outhouse...I screamed...He was so quick and fast. Like nothing happed. I don't remember seeing him after that." Unfortunately, the interviewer does not ask any follow-up questions as both interviewer and survivor were clearly too discomfited by the story.[82]

Accounts from Survivors Who Went into Hiding

Some of the most explicit descriptions of sexual assault come, perhaps surprisingly, from survivors who were able to flee from or find hiding places in Nazi occupied territory. These recollections also implicate a wider spectrum of non-Nazi collaborators and perpetrators. One, that of Claire G., even demonstrates the extent to which escaping Nazi oppression and ending up in Allied territory did not guarantee exemption from abuse.

Erika G. and her mother, Hungarian Jews, went into hiding while her father joined the Hungarian army. Eventually separated from her mother, Erika passed herself off as a maid, while hiding in various homes throughout the Hungarian countryside. According to her testimony, someone discovered she was concealing her identity, and she bought his silence by agreeing to work for him. This man had a wife and children, but, as she describes, he wanted "work in the bedroom." "He was annoyed that I was still a virgin, so he took care of that…that was a kind of bad experience to be subjected to sex that way and lose [my] virginity that way. I was saving it for the right man. I was only 22. By my standard that wasn't too high an age at the time. I was living kind of a sheltered life…I remember at midnight hearing the Hungarian national anthem. So for many years, every time I heard the anthem, it was very disturbing for me…"[83] The man abusing Erika never reported her to the authorities, but his wife wanted to, and Erika was forced to find another hiding place. Fortunately, she found refuge with a music teacher who had given her a scholarship years before. Erika was eventually reunited with her family after the war.

Phyllis L. recalls an incident in which the Polish farmer who was hiding her and a group of girls wanted to rape one of them: "We were at his mercy. Once he got drunk and he wanted to take Genka (a very pretty girl). Even though his wife and children were upstairs, he decided he wanted to make love with this girl. But Genka was always sick. That night they [the rest of the girls] said, if you do this, we leave. He got afraid that they would tell his wife. She would wonder why we are suddenly leaving…"[84] Living under false identity with a farm family near Brou, in France, Marie P. was sexually harassed by the man who took her in. "The people on the farm were nice, but strict…We used to eat pig all day, pig in the morning, pig in the day, pig at night. I remember eating that all the time…The man on the farm always wanted to put his hand under my blanket to wake me up. I knew if I told, I'd get thrown out. But I had to stay, until the end of the war…[I was] frightened of this man…"[85] Ruth P., who fled to Belgium and then to France during the war, was also molested by the man of the family who hid her. "He wanted me. The woman who was supposed to be his wife was his sister. I found this out much, much later. He molested me. It didn't go all the way. He didn't rape me. I didn't know what was going on. But I knew I didn't want to stay."[86]

Ida T., too, suffered abuse at the hands of a family who was ostensibly helping her. But her recounting is an example of what Lawrence Langer terms the divided self--a conscious effort to remain detached from the violation. "Something funny was going on there. There was only one bed. And we slept in one bed. The baby, too! It really bothered me. I was molested there. I couldn't take it any more. One day when the baby was sleeping and the wife was out, I left and went back to Stagniowice to my mother. I don't know what was going on there. Between the husband, the wife, and me. I know something was happening. I don't know what happened. If they included my in their sex acts. I just lived with it until today...blotted it out."[87]

Walter G., an Italian, witnessed the rape of his mother by German soldiers after their capture in the Cabruzzi mountains:

> "[We] went to another village and the Germans were there. [We were] told to go the German headquarters...My mother was taken away...I saw my mother briefly. I saw what certainly no human being should see, certainly not a young boy..."[88]

Walter's mother was allowed to rejoin her son after the incident, but Walter could not shake the traumatic image of his mother's violation. "She gave me her hand, which I refused. There was a little valley between mountains with golden wheat ripe for harvest. The golden wheat looked so beautiful. We walked silently. As I walked, a very dark snake went through my feet. I had a great phobia. That day has changed me forever. I haven't talked about this until recently. I made believe it didn't happen. Just before she died of cancer, she said, 'do you remember the time we were in the town?' and I said 'yes.' That's all that was said...Things were different though. Whether it was because I was different, I did feel it..."[89]

The testimonies of Eva S., Fela P., and Sara W. demonstrate that non-Nazi officials and resistance fighters were equally complicit in sexual assault and harassment. While hiding in the Czech town of Nitra, Eva S. was attacked by thugs from the fascist Hlinka Guard. She was hit repeatedly in the head by one of the men, forced to strip, and then beaten brutally with his baton. "[I was hit] twenty-five times on [my] bottom, and then twenty-five times behind my knee...[He] then pulled me up, pushed me up against the wall, pinched my breast. It hurt an awful lot. He kept saying, admit that you're Jewish. I wouldn't. He told [the other] soldiers to close the windows and put a silencer on [his] gun. He put it against my temple. '[This is] your last chance. I said 'I'm not Jewish.' He pushed me down the stairs." Her story ends here without offering further details, except to say that she was able to contact her parents after the attack.[90]

Fela P. refused to trade sexual favors with Soviet troops for food while fleeing through the USSR. "Four Russian soldiers...said to us, 'You want to go to town? We will provide you with food. A soldier could go to the head of the line in food queues...They said 'Stay the night.' I was very naïve. Four girls and four boys lying on the floor.

Every soldier took a girl. One started to kiss me. I was frightened. I wanted to go out. But the door was closed, and I didn't know where to go. I sat on a chair and fell asleep...The soldier wouldn't give me food..."[91]

Sara W., too, fended off the advances of Russian partisans. Initially living in the region of Poland that was occupied by the Soviet army, Sara, like so many other Jews, became engulfed by German forces after the launch of Operation Barbarossa in 1941. The Nazis executed her entire family, but she narrowly escaped after a non-Jewish friend came to her rescue. She soon joined a partisan group in the nearby forests. "I was in this group of Russians, males, and there was a shortage of women and they were all surprised that I wasn't willing to sleep with them. I just continued to say no and no and no...In the end, I had a routine. When the [male] was out for action, I'd sleep with a woman, whose partner was out, so that I wouldn't be alone, and I had a tent right next to the doctor and patients, so [I] was safe there..."[92] Sara was reunited with her aunt's family in Lodz after the war, and then, in an ironic twist, left Poland for Germany, where she married, had children. Ultimately, she opted to leave Europe altogether, settling in Australia.

The story of abuse did not begin for Clare G., a Polish girl whose family had moved to Germany in the 1920s, until she left for England as part of the Kindertransport. "I met these people in their liquor store. They looked like nice people. The first day, the man of the house said, 'Why don't you call whoever you want.' This man came in and started to touch me all over...I called my cousin. I should've called where my sister was. You didn't have such things in a Jewish home...I couldn't speak to anybody. That was a household that was helter-skelter. One day, I said to him, 'Aren't you ashamed? You are old enough to be my father. You have a daughter. He said, 'I don't want my daughter. I want you. I said, 'I was raised Orthodox.! I don't know such things!'" Clare's protests came to no avail. She was raped repeatedly by the man. "He came to the bedroom, put a hand over my mouth. 'If you say a word, I have people in big places. I will send you, your sister, and your brother back to Germany. I says, 'What did we do to you? He didn't care. He raped me. I was up all night. I took a bath. My God, what has happened to me? What can I do? This happened for quite a while. I was destroyed, totally destroyed."[93]

Clare was able to enlist the help of a local rabbi, who confronted her rapist. But in a disturbing twist of fate, it was Clare who stood accused of coming on to her assailant. Unable to tolerate the pain any longer, Clare escaped one night—accompanied by the man's daughter. After the war, she immigrated to the United States.[94]

Conclusion

Jewish women and men were victims of Nazi oppression on a number of levels, and the invasion of their sexual lives was but one weapon in an already sadistic arsenal. It is clear, as Gisela Bock points out, that "female members of the 'alien races' were murdered as women, as givers of life, child bearers and mothers of the next generation of their people."[95]   One cannot even begin to ponder the collective trauma inflicted on an entire generation of teenage women— trauma that knew no national boundaries, trauma that cut to the core of what it meant to be a woman.   Jewish men, again many of them children and teenagers, were also victims of sexual abuse, if not actually in the violations they endured at the hands of camp powerbrokers and guards, then in the maiming they carried out on their bodies to conceal their Jewishness.   In the following chapter, we will see how even "positive" recollections of sexual behavior during the Holocaust bear a similar mark of collective distress.

Notes

1 Bradley Smith and Agnes Peterson, eds., *Heinrich Himmler: Geheimreden 1933 bis 1945* (Frankfurt, 1974).

2 Ringelheim, "The Split Between Gender and the Holocaust," in Dalia Ofer and Lenore Weitzman, eds., *Women in the Holocaust* (New Haven, 1998), 344.

3 Joan Ringelheim, "The Holocaust: Taking Women into Account," *Jewish Quarterly* (Autumn 1992): 22. See also Ringelheim, "Women and the Holocaust: A Reconsideration of Research," in Carol Rittner and John Roth, eds., *Different Voices: Women and the Holocaust* (New York, 1993); Mary Lowenthal Felstiner, *To Paint Her Life: Charlotte Solomon in the Nazi Era* (New York, 1994); and Raul Hilberg, "Men and Women," in *Perpetrators, Victims, Bystanders* (New York, 1992).

4 Marlene Heinemann, *Gender and Destiny: Women Writers and the Holocaust* (Westport, Conn., 1986), 15, and Joan Ringelheim, "Women and the Holocaust: A Reconsideration of Research."

5 Sara Horowitz, "Women in Holocaust Literature: Engendering Trauma Memory," in *Women in the Holocaust*, 365, 376.

6 Testimony of Toby K., Testimony Number 30719, Survivors of the Shoah Visual History Foundation, West Orange, United States, 8 July 1997, 02:00:10:16-02:05:11:29.

7 Testimony of Magda S., Testimony Number 18057, Survivors of the Shoah Visual History Foundation, Hallandale, United States, 1 August, 1996, 03:12:46:21-03:15:08:03.

8 Testimony of Martha V., Testimony Number 33145, Survivors of the Shoah Visual History Foundation, Toronto, Canada, 20 August 1997, 03:19:27:28-03:23:04:1.

9 Testimony of Jean S., Testimony Number 32842, Survivors of the Shoah Visual History Foundation, Jenkintown, United States, 7 August 1997, 02:23:27:14-02:26:37:01.

10 Testimony of Mary W, Testimony Number 8123, Survivors of the Shoah Visual History Foundation, North Bergen, United States, 30 October 1995, 05:00:13:20-05:12:15:24.

11 Testimony of Eva S., Testimony Number 23853, Survivors of the Shoah Visual History Foundation, West Roxbury, United States, 2 December 1996, 04:10:41:21-04:14:37:20.

12 Ruth Schwertfeger, *Women of Theresienstadt: Voices from a Concentration Camp* (New York, 1989), 61

[13] Testimony of Irena S., Testimony Number 30898, Survivors of the Shoah Visual History Foundation, San Francisco, United States, 19 July 1997, 02:15:08-02:20:35.

[14] Testimony of Emil N., Testimony Number 16680, Survivors of the Shoah Visual History Foundation, Mount Vernon, United States, 20 January 1997, 02:17:50-02:20:51.

[15] Testimony of Rena G., Testimony Number 19221, Survivors of the Shoah Visual History Foundation, Farmington Hills, United States, 30 August 1996, 02:16:15-2:20-:18; 05:00:44-05:04:18.

[16] Testimony of Germaine P., Testimony Number 33265, Survivors of the Shoah Visual History Foundation, Clearwater, United States, 7 September 1997, 02:21:53:23-02:29:41:19.

[17] Testimony of Janos S., Testimony Number 18090, Survivors of the Shoah Visual History Foundation, Las Vegas, United States, 1 August 1996, Hungary 1928, 03:26:17:24-04:02:00:29.

[18] Testimony of Helene U., Testimony Number 20200, Survivors of the Shoah Visual History Foundation, Brooklyn, United States, 26 September 1996, 02:27:13:00-03:06:35:22.

[19] Testimony of Linda M., Testimony Number 17987, Survivors of the Shoah Visual History Foundation, West Woodmere, United States, 31 July 1, 1996, 02:19:20:21-02:22:22:21.

[20] Testimony of Fanny L., Testimony Number 42751, Survivors of the Shoah Visual History Foundation, 05:01:00:26-05:06:24:09.

[21] Testimony of Herta M., Testimony Number 18043, Engelwood, United States, 31 July 1996, 02:15:29:21-02:21:02:29.

[22] Testimony of Eva S., Testimony Number 21666, Cote St. Luc, United States, 25 October 1996, 03:19:51:03-03:24:47:19.

[23] Testimony of Shary N., Testimony Number 21203, Survivors of the Shoah Visual History Foundation, Sarasota, United States, 22 October 1996, 03:18:30:10-03:21:17:08.

[24] Testimony of Magdalena V., Testimony Number 18311, Survivors of the Shoah Visual History Foundation, Port Charlotte, United States, 7 August 1996, 03:07:05:12-03:12:33:25.

[25] Testimony of Nellie A., Testimony Number 30733, Survivors of the Shoah Visual History Foundation, Toronto, Canada, 7 July 1997, 03:00:08-03:04:12.

[26] Testimony of Chasia K., Testimony Number 34767, Survivors of the Shoah Visual History Foundation, Tel Aviv, Israel, 28 September 1997, 02:03:35-02:10:01.

[27] Testimony of Luba L., Testimony Number 34921, Survivors of the Shoah Visual History Foundation, Stockton, United States, 2 November 1997, 03:16:32-03:25:32.

[28] Testimony of Benesch T., Testimony Number 25895, Survivors of the Shoah Visual History Foundation, Walled Lake, United States, 10 February 1997, 03:09:22-03:15:09.

[29] Testimony of Lennie J., Testimony Number 23717, Survivors of the Shoah Visual History Foundation, Ventura, United States, 02:07:00:10-02:13:27:02.

[30] Testimony of Bronka K., Testimony Number 29421, Survivors of the Shoah Visual History Foundation, Toronto, Canada, 30 May 1997, 04:20:03:21-04:27:14:23.

[31] Ibid.

[32] Ibid.

[33] Heinemann, 19.

[34] Testimony of Sabina M., Testimony Number 17323, Survivors of the Shoah Visual History Foundation Los Angeles, United States, 7 July 1996, 03:11:19:20-03:15:57:20.

[35] Testimony of Sarah W., Testimony Number 27204, Survivors of the Shoah Visual History Foundation, Flushing, United States, 13 March 1997, 04:07:18:00-04:11:03:06.

[36] Testimony of Eva S., Testimony Number 21666, Survivors of the Shoah Visual History Foundation, Cote St. Luc, United States, 25 October 1996, 04:00:08:06-04:05:36:07.

[37] Testimony of Doba A., Testimony Number 29753, Survivors of the Shoah Visual History Foundation, Melbourne, Australia, 28 March 1997, 04:07:40:14-04:09:16:06.

[38] Testimony of Luba S., Testimony Number 18672, Survivors of the Shoah Visual History Foundation, Monticello, United States, 16 August 1996, 03:17:31:22-03:22:25:04.

[39] Testimony of Golda N., Testimony Number 30054, Survivors of the Shoah Visual History Foundation, Toronto, Canada, 19 June 1997, 05:02:53:18-05:05:54:11.

[40] Testimony of Phyllis P., Testimony Number 24202, Survivors of the Shoah Visual History Foundation, Delray Beach, United States, 16 December 1996, 02:06:34:07-02:11:04:05. For her part, Huguette F. contends that the Nazis put something in her soup, and Helene U. says that it was the food that caused her to stop menstruating. Testimony of Huguette F., Testimony Number 24766, Survivors of the Shoah Visual History Foundation, Brookline, United States, 21 January 1997, 02:25:45:17-03:01:12:00; Testimony of Helene U., Testimony Number 20200, Survivors of the Shoah Visual History Foundation, Brooklyn, United States, 21 September 1996, 03:06:35:22-03:11:10:09.

[41] Testimony of Joan W., Testimony Number 20213, Survivors of the Shoah Visual History Foundation, Miami, United States, 27 September 1996, 02:02:45:07-02:07:06:11.

[42] Testimony of Rachela P., Testimony Number 27003, Survivors of the Shoah Visual History Foundation, Melbourne, Australia, 26 January 1997, 04:13:06:13-04:15:25:21.

[43] Testimony of Greta K., Testimony Number 26524, Survivors of the Shoah Visual History Foundation, San Francisco, United States, 3 March 1997, 02:15:58-02:19:06.

[44] Testimony of Dresla S., Testimony Number 34416, Survivors of the Shoah Visual History Foundation, New York, United States, 7 October 1997, 03:24:33-03:27:20.

[45] Testimony of Bianka K., Testimony Number 13723, Survivors of the Shoah Visual History Foundation, Oakville, Canada, 29 March 1996, 3:27:10-4:02:32.

[46] Testimony of Bebe F., Testimony Number 33191, Survivors of the Shoah Visual History Foundation, 8 September 1997, 03:14:00:00-03:19:20:00.

[47] Testimony of Hanka C., Testimony Number 34766, Survivors of the Shoah Visual History Foundation, Melbourne, Australia, November 1997, 02:22:59:29-02:27:25:00.

[48] Testimony of Ibolya S., Survivors of the Shoah Visual History Foundation, Toronto, Canada, 18 June 1997.

[49] Testimony of Herta M., Testimony Number 18043, Survivors of the Shoah Visual History Foundation, Engelwood, United States, 31 July 1996, 02:15:29:21-02:21:02:29.

[50] Testimony of Abraham B., Testimony Number 18061, Survivors of the Shoah Visual History Foundation, 14 August 1996, 04:03:23:28-04:09:04:15.

[51] Vera Laska, "Women in the Resistance and in the Holocaust," in *Different Voices*, 266.

[52] Testimony of Rachel D., Testimony Number 18294, Survivors of the Shoah Visual History Foundation, North Caufield, 5 August 1996, 03:02:15:22-03:04:01:06.

[53] Testimony of Alex C., Testimony Number 20021, Survivors of the Shoah Visual History Foundation, Livingston, United States, 24 September 1996, no time code.

[54] Testimony of William D., Testimony Number 32569, Survivors of the Shoah Visual History Foundation, East Brighton, United States, 16 June 1997, no time code.

[55] Heineiman, 16.

[56] Ibid., 27, 28.

[57] Testimony of Inge F., Testimony Number 11083, Survivors of the Shoah Visual History Foundation, Brooklyn, United States, 18 January 1996, 03:19:00-03:24:47.

[58] Testimony of Bina W., Testimony Number 33960, Survivors of the Shoah Visual History Foundation, Melbourne, Australia, 6 August 1997, 02:09:47-02:12:25.

[59] Testimony of Mina L., Testimony Number 18757, Survivors of the Shoah Visual History Foundation, Philadelphia, United States, 20 August 1996, 01:26:43-02:02:31.

[60] Testimony of Dana S., Testimony Number 14894, Survivors of the Shoah Visual History Foundation, Beverly Hills, United States, 7 May 1996, 02:06:39-02:11:51.

[61] Testimony of Bernard Z., Testimony Number 35123, Survivors of the Shoah Visual History Foundation, Martinez, United States, 2 November 1997, 03:05:12-03:08:09.

[62] Testimony of Imre H., Testimony Number 8500, Survivors of the Shoah Visual History Foundation, Downsview, Canada, 9 November 1995, 1:13:02-1:17:44.

[63] Testimony of Malka W., Testimony Number 42723, Survivors of the Shoah Visual History Foundation, Allentown, United States, 28 May 1998, 2:03:09-2:05:58.

[64] Testimony of Paula H., Testimony Number 33422, Survivors of the Shoah Visual History Foundation, Cote St. Luc, Canada, 15 September 1997, 02:19:11-02:21:20.

[65] Charles Roland, *Courage Under Siege: Starvation, Disease, and Death in the Warsaw Ghetto* (New York, 1992), 49.

[66] Ibid., and Alan Adelson and Robert Lapides, eds., *Lodz Ghetto: Inside a Community Under Siege* (New York, 1989), pp. 526, 44.

[67] Testimony of Sigmund T., Testimony Number 35109, Survivors of the Shoah Visual History Foundation, Teaneck, United States, 30 October 1997, 04:03:31:24-04:06:00:26.

[68] Testimony of Rita H., Testimony Number 30717, Survivors of the Shoah Visual History Foundation, Silver Spring, United States, 2 July 1997, 2:13:10-2:14:59.

[69] Testimony of Gina L., Testimony Number 31586, Survivors of the Shoah Visual History Foundation, Montreal , Canada, 1 August 1997, 02:19:09-02:23:51.

[70] See Solomon Bloom, "Dictator of the Lodz Ghetto: The Strange History of Mordecai Chaim Rumkowski," in Michael Marrus, ed., *The Nazi Holocaust: Historical Articles on the Destruction of European Jews* (Westport, 1989), Vol. 6, p. 299, and Leonard Tushnet, *Pavement of Hell* (New York, 1972), p. 69. While Bloom avers that Rumkowski "was wide open to the temptations of the flesh," Tushnet recounts only that Rumkowski, after having been a widower, took a much younger woman as his bride.

[71] Testimony of Shary N., Testimony Number 21203, Survivors of the Shoah Visual History Foundation, Sarasota, United States, 22 October 1996, 03:13:03:29-03:16:46:06.

[72] Testimony of Deborah S., Testimony Number 25384, Survivors of the Shoah Visual History Foundation, Vallejo, United States, 31 January 1997, 05:02:44:02-05:04:32:17.

[73] Testimony of Bronia S., Testimony Number 10747, Survivors of the Shoah Visual History Foundation, 01:22:37:05-01:25:50:20.

[74] Vera Laska, "Women in the Resistance and in the Holocaust," in *Different Voices*, 263-266.

[75] Olga Lengyel, "Scientific Experiments," in *Different Voices*, 126.

[76] Testimony of Coenraad R., Testimony Number 18548, Survivors of the Shoah Visual History Foundation, Sherman Oaks, United States, 19 August 1996, 05:24:13:02-05:27:58:27.

[77] Testimony of Hermann S., Testimony Number 14480, Survivors of the Shoah Visual History Foundation, Chesterfield, United States, 28 April 1996, 06:00.

[78] Ibid.

[79] Testimony of Harry B., Testimony Number 33336, Survivors of the Shoah Visual History Foundation, Staten Island, United States, 14 August 1997, 06:10:31:01-06:15:37:18.

[80] Testimony of Nathan O., Testimony Number 20084, Survivors of the Shoah Visual History Foundation, New Hyde Park, United States, 11 August 1996, 03:07-03:13.

[81] Testimony of Eugene L., Testimony Number 28052, Survivors of the Shoah Visual History Foundation, Brooklyn, United States, 13 April 1997, 02:13:37:08-02:19:14:15.

[82] Testimony of Douglas F., Testimony Number 29788, Survivors of the Shoah Visual History Foundation, Baltimore, United States, 2 June 1997, 02:16:43:12-02:21:31:10.

[83] Testimony of Erika G., Testimony Number 25797, Survivors of the Shoah Visual History Foundation, Los Angeles, United States, 14 February 1997, 02:20:44:01-02:27:08:27.

[84] Testimony of Phyllis L., Testimony Number 31585, Survivors of the Shoah Visual History Foundation, Deer Park, United States, 31 July 1997, 04:15:49:28-04:21:03:27.

[85] Testimony of Marie P., Testimony Number 33263, Survivors of the Shoah Visual History Foundation, Melbourne, Australia, 7 September 1997, 02:07:15:24-02:10:59:13.

[86] Testimony of Ruth P., Testimony Number 19973, Survivors of the Shoah Visual History Foundation, San Clemente, United States, 7 September 1996, 03:09:15:05-03:15:41:07.

[87] Testimony of Ida T., Testimony Number 7712, Survivors of the Shoah Visual History Foundation, Cranbury, United States, 18 October 1995, 02:00:08:09-02:04:22:20.

---

[88] Testimony of Walter G., Testimony Number 33330, Survivors of the Shoah Visual History Foundation, Airmont, United States, 14 August 1997, 04:11:40:15-04:22:59:11.

[89] Ibid.

[90] Testimony of Eva S., Testimony Number 33024, Survivors of the Shoah Visual History Foundation, Caufield, United States, 24 July 1997, 04:15:05:26-04:22:38:10.

[91] Testimony of Fela P., Testimony Number 33606, Survivors of the Shoah Visual History Foundation, Ormond, United States, 2 July 1997, 03:02:40:26-03:09:02:16.

[92] Testimony of Sara W., Testimony Number 19447, Survivors of the Shoah Visual History Foundation, Toorak, Australia, 2 September 1996, 02:18:55:02-02:24:19:11.

[93] Testimony of Clare G., Testimony Number 24434, Survivors of the Shoah Visual History Foundation, New York, United States, 2 January 1997, 02:15:19:03-02:20:35:24.

[94] Ibid.

[95] Gisela Bock, "'Equality,' 'Difference,' and 'Inferiority:' Motherhood, Antenatalism, and Gender Relations in National Socialist Racism," (unpublished manuscript), 32.

Chapter 3

"Consensual" Sex, Deep Memory, and Working Through

One of the ever present dangers of Holocaust research and writing is the affixing of uplift and hope where there was, and perhaps is, none to be found. Lawrence Langer's warning is apt: "The need to make the Holocaust appear more harmless than it was has many roots, and hence many branches, leaves, and blossoms. Its efforts to sweeten the bitter fruits of mass murder will have to be monitored for decades, and perhaps generations, if we are to prevent what happened from slipping into a vague limbo of forgetfulness, a footnote to contemporary history instead of the central historical moment of our time..."[1] Dominick LaCapra similarly inveighs against a response that "circumvents, denies, or represses the trauma that called it into existence, for example, through unqualified objectification, formal analysis, or harmonizing, indeed redemptive narrative through which one derives from the suffering of others something career enhancing, 'spiritually uplifting,' or identity forming for oneself or one's group."[2]

While I agree that Holocaust history, documentary, and exhibition work frequently employs a "trope of comedy," I am wary of imposing a monolithic nihilism on all survivor commentary. This is especially true for memories of sexual behavior, courtships, and weddings. Yet a closer reading of Langer might lead to an alternate conclusion, namely that these memories are no less real than those of degradation, but that they, as common memories, are invariably scarred by some "deeper," traumatic memory. My research into survivor testimonies of "consensual" sexual activity during the Holocaust, a "choiceless choice" in so many respects, adds nuance to this premise. As I mentioned in the introduction, however, there is little intellectual guidance in addressing survivor memories of sexuality and intimacy in the ghettos, camps, and hiding places. Sybil Milton echoes Des Pres in decrying the mythologizing of survivor sexual behavior: "A popular postwar myth, sometimes exploited and sensationalized, held that Jewish women were forced to serve as prostitutes in the SS bordellos and were frequently raped. Although such cases did undoubtedly occur, it was not the norm and reflects a macabre postwar misuse of the Holocaust for popular titillation. Sexuality, either heterosexual or lesbian, was most likely practiced by prisoners who were camp functionaries and therefore better fed..."[3] Like Des Pres, Milton goes on to mention numerous aspects of sexual activity among individuals in the ghettos and camps:

> ...clandestine liaisons did occur, even in Auschwitz, where men were assigned to labor details in women's camps. Brief stolen moments were arranged in potato storage sheds, clothing depots, warehouses, laundry vans, the bakery, the canteen, and even in the chicken coops...In Gurs, a limited number of passes were allotted to each barracks so that women could visit their interned husbands in the men's enclosure, and although privacy was hard to find in Theresienstadt, lovers met hurriedly in the barracks' coal bunker at night. Weddings also took place in Theresienstadt and other ghettos and transit camps where milder conditions prevailed; and if both spouses survived, these symbolic marriages were often legalized in postwar civil ceremonies. There were also deep friendships between women that may have become lesbian relationships. These have been difficult to document given the inhibitions of survivors and historians. Occasionally, flirtation and sex were used to buy food or a better work situation.[4]

Olga Lengyel, a survivor of Auschwitz, puts it succinctly: "Even in the shadow of the crematory the emotions could not be entirely suppressed. Love, or what passed for it in the degraded atmosphere of the death camp, was but a distortion of what it is for normal people, for society in Birkenau was but a distortion of normal human society.[5]

Charles Roland, in his monograph on the Warsaw ghetto, also weaves in and out of ambivalent assertions about sexual behavior. In the same breath that he claims a negative impact on sexuality by ghetto life, he admits that there were numerous cases of girls who became sexually active precisely because of their desperate situation:

> Sexuality was commonly affected negatively by ghetto life. Sex is central to the thoughts, desires, and well-being of most of us. It is also an activity likely to have been disrupted by the severe physical and psychological pressures of life under Nazi rule. But attitudes toward sexuality were ambivalent...Although the grossly inadequate ration probably had an anti-aphrodisiac effect, and certainly caused some impotence as well as lack of interest—a phenomenon much commented upon by prisoner of war camps, though there the disinclination was usually reinforced by a total absence of women, again one must keep in mind the differences among the ghetto population. At any given time, while many were starving and perhaps were indifferent to sexuality, many others, better fed, felt the usual psychological urges. Moreover, these urges may have been felt at an earlier age, or indulged earlier, than had been the case before the war...Many so-called nice girls, who would never have engaged in sexual relations out of wedlock before the war, did so in the ghetto. 'Nobody liked to admit it seriously, but the atmosphere there was one of anxious expectation of the ultimate fate, and sex seemed a way to become immortal...' [6]

For their part, Dalia Ofer and Felicja Karay focus on the extent to which sex was manipulated for survival in both the ghettos and camps. Ofer mentions numerous diaries that refer to prostitution in the ghettos as well as liaisons with influential men on the Jewish councils or in the ghetto police.[7] Karay, writing on women in the forced labor camps, recounts an incident in the work camp attached to Majdanek, where a wife "chose to obtain food and money in the accepted manner" to save his life. Horrified by what his wife had done, the man refused to eat and was near death before other inmates nursed him back to health.[8]

What I have found in my examination of hundreds of testimonies confirms much of what is said about sexual behavior among survivors during the Holocaust—except that it was more widespread than has been admitted. If we situate survivor discussions of sexuality in different settings (ghetto, camp, hiding) we find numerous and correspondingly diverse experiences. Although many facets of life in both environments were roughly comparable--the disease, starvation, arbitrary killing, and lack of privacy, there are more discussions, in the oral testimonies surveyed for this study, of consensual sex, weddings, and marriages in the ghettos and hiding places than in the camps. The reasons for this are obvious. In the camps, men and women were incarcerated separately, but in the ghettos and hiding places, families or what could pass as a family unit, basically remained intact, allowing for the possibility of men and women to pursue intimacy.

Weddings and Marriages

Wedding ceremonies, in most survivor recollections, were small, improvised affairs, with makeshift *chupas* and wedding cakes. The description of one wedding in particular, that of Tola and Jack H. inside the Lodz ghetto, is curious because husband and wife chose to emphasize different elements in their interviews. Tola essentially focused on the food served, a piece of bread, potato peels, and coffee dregs, but Jack expounded on the origins of their relationship. "[Tola] was sixteen when I met her. She was beautiful. Her mother was always hollering [at her], 'So, you want to go with the big boys!'[9]   At Margarete W.'s wedding in Hamburg, food was so scarce that they made dishes from castor oil.[10]

The marriage ceremonies of Lennie J. and David L. were conducted with utmost concern over secrecy. Before the Nazi invasion of the Netherlands, Lennie became romantically involved with a rabbi. "I was seeing the rabbi of the town, and we were getting engaged...He was older than I was, but he fell in love with me and we got engaged." After the German occupation, Lennie's father secured a hiding place for the family, but he insisted that his daughter and her paramour get married before they went into hiding together. "So we went to city hall, very quietly and got married...I had no dress...I used a curtain from a window as a veil..."[11]   David, meanwhile, hid in a villa on the outskirts of Warsaw sometime in 1943. The owner of the villa was a Gentile woman, a "Mrs. Mochska." David was accompanied into hiding by his girlfriend, whose father, a jeweler, insisted that the two get married before they lived in a house together. Risking discovery, and fearing denunciation by the ex-husband of the woman hiding them (a recurrent theme with survivors), David and his fiancée threw caution to the wind and had a small wedding celebration, attended by nineteen friends. As he remembers, they had cupcakes to eat. Both he and his wife survived the war, and after a brief period in a displaced persons' camp, the two left Europe for the United States.[12]

Asking survivors why they married elicits diverse responses, some of which have very little to do with romance. Irena S. says that she ran off to get married when the Nazis began liquidating the Warsaw ghetto because her boyfriend had "protective" papers from the Jewish community.[13] Solomon K., who was married in Kovno, also recalls that, although he fell in love with his future wife when he was twelve and she was thirteen, they did not decide to marry until it became clear that police in the ghetto were selecting single people for deportation in greater numbers.[14] And Freda P. remembers that she chose to marry her boyfriend in the Plonsk ghetto for very practical reasons: "One day, we got the idea that if we got married, we would have a place to stay [in the ghetto]...We would get a corner to a room..."[15]

Memories attributing marriage solely to romance, however, are abundant. Emil N., for one, has such a recollection of his courtship to his girlfriend, Regina: "What I did, it seemed it was right at the time. I did it because I loved her. Maybe she did it because she knew I wanted her...[all I said] I'm taking you for my wife. That was about all."[16] Rachel D. too admits that "people were wondering--you're getting married in the ghetto? [But] We were very much in love."[17] A native of Lithuania, Sonia F. met her future husband David at a concert in March 1941, two months before the German invasion. While standing in line to buy tickets, David, suddenly struck by this mysterious and charming woman, offered to pay the price of her ticket. Although she refused, and never paid him any mind, she saw him frequently at work and then, by chance again, at a wedding, where she agreed to dance with him. In her words, "we danced all night long."[18]

Passing under a false identity in a small French town, Cecile K. hid with the aunt of her future husband. "When I met my husband...I kind of fell in love with him, and he had all kinds of ladies..."[19]One of the more curious memories comes from George B., a survivor who married in the Shanghai ghetto.[20] He recounts that he met his future wife in a theater. (She apparently kept grabbing his leg.) Their wedding was complicated by the fact that his newfound girlfriend was a widow and hence, under Jewish law, obliged to marry her dead husband's brother. The two opted out of an Orthodox ceremony as a result.[21]

One characteristic shared by survivor memories of life affirming events such as marriage is contrast—or what Langer might see as a layering of common and deep memory. This quality of memory is pronounced in recollections of courtships, weddings, and marriages in the ghettos, hiding places, and to a lesser extent, displaced persons' camps. Descriptions of wedding ceremonies in the ghettos, for instance, are often followed by stories of loss. Marc R., who married his childhood sweetheart in Radom in 1943, remembers that he initially opposed the idea of marriage in the context of the deportations. At first fearing that he would leave his wife a widow, he eventually came around to the idea of marriage when it seemed that neither would survive and that neither had anything to lose. Indeed, as Marc describes, six weeks after their wedding, he and his wife were sent to Majdanek.[22] (Both survived the camps and were reunited after the war). Chana W. was not as lucky. She remembers that during the night before her family's deportation from Munkacevo in Czechoslovakia, she slept between her parents in a small bed and held her mother's hands. She recalls that her father said quietly to her mother, "If I had to marry you again, I would." She immediately follows with two brief yet anguished statements: "It was the last night in the ghetto," and "My mother was very pretty."[23] Paula P. remembered a boy she planned to marry in the ghetto in Rszeszow: "[We] didn't go out much, just stayed in the house, talking about school, food. I had my first kiss...Henry. They're all dead."[24] Irena S. was married in the Warsaw ghetto, and on her wedding night, she opted to stay with her new husband rather than have a cup of tea with her mother, which she had done regularly before and during her courtship. The day after her wedding, Irena discovered that her mother had been deported. With this memory firmly embedded in her mind, she admits that she can never disassociate her wedding night from her mother's death.[25]

Hanka C. and Jenny C. relate stories of lovers who perished—hiding, in the case of Hanka, or fighting with partisans, in the case of Jenny. Hanka was torn between two suitors, Eli and Itche, before she went into hiding in a bunker near Zelechow in Poland. "I [didn't] know what to do. I pushed everyone away." Eli, Hanka's father, and her two brothers found a different hiding place, but towards the end of the war, they were discovered and executed. In 1944, Hanka returned to Zelechow and was reunited with Itche. The two married, and after the war left for Germany and then Australia.[26]

Not even sixteen when the Nazis launched their invasion of Soviet territory in June 1941, Jenny C. joined an underground resistance cell and experienced both passion and tragedy in the love of her life, David Yochai, the leader of her unit. In between small acts of sabotage, the two found time for harmless diversions like tango dancing and reminiscing over their once normal lives. She once told David that she wished she had been a dog instead of a Jew—because Germans "didn't hurt dogs." When, in March 1943, the Nazis liquidated the Swiencyany ghetto in which Jenny's parents were trapped, Jenny couldn't bear the thought of leaving her family to what was, in her mind, certain death. On her mother's admonition, however, she escaped the confines of the ghetto, only to be arrested shortly thereafter because she was in possession of a bar of soap. Sent to the ghetto in Vilna, Jenny worked on a farm and planned an escape. She disguised herself as a peasant girl (wearing rouge—apparently something Jewish girls never did, and carrying her shoes to prevent wearing them down), and then hid on a passenger train. Eventually, she stumbled upon a particular resistance unit, the Chapayev brigade, and was reunited with her lover, David, who was fighting with another group. The brief outburst of joy proved short-lived; David was killed in a hail of gunfire when German troops overran his unit. Jenny, although wounded in a pitched battle, was able to recover and survive the war.[27]

Most of the Shoah Foundation testimonies which I viewed that relate to marriage in displaced persons' camps accentuate themes of hope and survival, either by choice of the survivor or by design of the interviewer. Arie T., a Rumanian Jew, was deported to Auschwitz in 1944. He lost his entire family there. And yet in his interview, he clings to positive memories: After the war, he was reunited with an old girlfriend while travelling through Budapest. "We just…run into each other. She found me and wouldn't let go…" After spending a couple of years in a displaced persons' camp, the couple immigrated to Palestine and married.[28] Sally S. also holds on to uplifting thoughts as her way of working through the trauma of her wartime experience. She lost most of her family in the death camps in Poland (she herself was in Auschwitz and Bergen Belsen). After the war, she was reunited with a friend from Tomaszaw (in Poland), whom she married—moving eventually through the DP camps to the United States.[29]

Other survivors describe, in much the same way, the relationships they cultivated with their future spouses in the DP camps. In the Feldafing DP camp, Helen G., a survivor of Auschwitz and Stutthof, met the man who would become her future husband. "Was it love at first sight? I don't know, I was too young, too naïve, but he never let me out of his sight..."[30] Rose H., also met her future mate in Feldafing: "...[He] came everyday to visit [me] and kept saying that his mother would love him to have a girl like 'Rose'..."[31] In the Eschwege DP camp, Basia W. fell in love and got married. "I bought a pair of light shoes, summer shoes...We were married on Valentine's Day..."[32] Mala G. had an on again, off again relationship with a man in a camp after the war: "If you knew him for a few days or weeks, you'd get married, but I was sheltered and didn't do what I was supposed to...I kept breaking up with him [Abe]...I was impulsive. If he would come up to me, he'd get so much on my nerves. I've got a temper. But I was touched with the love thing..."[33] Dresla S., on her wedding in Heidenheim DP camp: "Someone...said, the best fitting couple was Dresla and Ezra...The whole camp came to the wedding. I cooked. From a different town, a rabbi came and performed the ceremony."[34] Mania L., also an Auschwitz survivor, is short and simple when describing her wedding in the Eichstatt DP camp. 'He was the only single man...[We got] married in 1947...[We] had a chupa. I made pickled tongue..."[35]

Two of the survivors, however, emphasize what was ultimately for them an ironic occasion, a wedding celebration in a camp in the wake of the destruction of their entire families. Minna A.'s future husband played in the orchestra in the Landsberg DP camp. He wanted to play at their wedding, but she said, "No." "I lost my parents. I didn't want any music, but...they still played...Somebody got married before me, and I borrowed the dress from her. Everything was borrowed...I was lucky, very lucky, let me tell you..."[36] Eva L. offered this disappointing epitaph to her wedding in Bad Salzschlirf DP camp: "I didn't take any pictures of it...I have nothing to show for it..."[37]

"Consensual Sex" in the Ghettos and in Hiding

There are patterns which emerge from survivor discussions of "consensual" sex that cut across milieu and gender (to the extent that we can talk of something like "consensual" in an environment where only abnormal exigencies applied.) Most of the conversations of sex as "romance" come from survivors with ghetto or hiding experiences, and most of these survivors tend to be men who were teenagers at the time. From Sol. R. we have the following reminiscence of the Warsaw ghetto:

> One day, in a surprise, I was assigned to a barracks outside the ghetto. I became a handyman for a German office, because I knew some German. I was a pretty good size boy, strong at 15. This German officer had a daughter, about the same age, maybe 16. Her name was Amy. She got to like me. I didn't realize the consequences, what could happen. I taught her how to dance...Half the time I didn't work. I was schmoozing most of the time with her. All the Jews working with me started to get worried. [They said], 'here's Sol fooling around with the commander's daughter.' I made love to her. She told me she wanted me to run away to her grandfather's farm in Germany. She was like--'no-one has to know if you're Jewish.' Amy got a little too close to me. Every night, the Germans would party. Amy arranged for me to take the star off and have me serve at these [parties]. The Poles who served with me knew that I was Jewish, but they couldn't speak German like I could. I'd dance with Amy and dance with her mother. One day, a 30 year old Jewish man in the barracks took me aside and said, 'you're gonna get us killed--cut it out!' I didn't realize the consequences, when you're having a good time as a young boy.[38]

Later, during a smuggling run, Sol was taken in by a Polish family outside the walls of the ghetto, where he began another liaison with the daughter.[39] The two stories appear incredible, and they may in fact be embellishments or fiction; that cannot be determined from the interview. Still, it is clear that for Sol, his image as a "Casanova," whether real or imagined, empowers him as he confronts the otherwise horrible reality of his wartime experience.

While survivors who discuss consenting intimacy come from a variety of localities, a large number are from Jews who were interned in Theresienstadt, or Terezin, the so-called "model, or paradise ghetto" located some forty miles north of Prague. According to Norbert Troller, "...in Theresienstadt, the ghetto, there were numerically as many men as there were women, of all ages, tightly crowded together, but separated in barracks under primitive living conditions, starving, working hard, living on borrowed time. They were relatively unguarded but not free, although they did not have to worry about the basic necessities and thus the idea of sex could not be far off. Only a very few had the privilege of living and sleeping in seclusion together. The rest of us found ways and means to enjoy, however fleetingly, the blissful intimacy between lovers..."[40]

Kurt T. and Dina B., offer these substantiating experiences of Theresienstadt:

> [Kurt T.]...In Terezin, we were herded into a stable. I don't remember if there was a toilet. The next morning, there was, sleeping in the other side of the isle, there was a guy married with his wife. It was not bragging. It was rather expressing a spirit of defiance when he told me that he made love to his wife three times. It was a way of saying, 'Hitler can't do anything to us...'[41]

> [Dina B.]...Karel became the love of my life. This completely changed my life. I was nineteen when I got there [Terezin.] I had had many platonic boyfriends, maybe kissing, but I never had a person about whom I could say I cared more than myself. Karel felt the same way about me. Every free moment we had, we were together, and when we weren't together, we automatically thought about each other...[42]

Dina became separated from Karel after their deportation to Auschwitz. (Karel eventually perished in the camp). Unaware of his fate, Dina struck up a romance with a kapo named Willie while working as an assistant to her Block Elder. After meeting Dina for the first time, Willie began sending a series of love notes. She still thought of Karel but admits, "This was a different planet." In her testimony, she remembers laughing uncontrollably when Willie would kiss her because he was missing his molars, and he reminded her of a rabbit. She insists, however, that the relationship did not progress beyond kissing, at least initially. Her affection for Willie grew when she discovered that he gave food to several women who were pregnant—to no avail; these women and their babies were all sent to the gas chambers.[43] Dina and Willie's relationship eventually became a sexual one, but she was frightened of the possibility of becoming pregnant. She had already undergone an abortion in Theresienstadt and made doubly sure that Willie was "always really careful." As with Karel, though, Dina was to be separated from her second love once the Nazis evacuated the inmates from the camp in January 1945.[44]

Recollections of sexual activity in hiding can be found in the testimonies of Ernst S., Mark N., and Frank S., all of whom were in their twenties during the war. Ernst S. went into hiding in Germany in 1943 by assuming the identity of a non-Jewish school friend. He tried to flee to Switzerland but was arrested (luckily by Swiss authorities) and interned in various Swiss camps until 1944. After the war, he left for the United States. He alludes to a relationship he had with a female notary ("...very much in need of love...") who helped him get the papers he needed to go into hiding.[45]   Mark N. lived under a false identity in Czechoslovakia where he was arrested for selling religious effects featuring the signature of the Pope. Fleeing his captors, he became romantically involved with a non-Jewish women to whom he feared revealing his Jewish identity. "[She was] a nice girl, fine girl, but only Jews were circumcised, so I couldn't fool around...She was very shy. One day, I had a date with her. She was told to find out if I was Jewish...[I said] I couldn't be unfaithful to my love..." It was only after the war, when he saw this woman again, that she discovered his true identity.[46]   Frank S. also went into hiding in Czechoslovakia in 1944. His description of his love affair is curt but evocative: "Anna's father was a drunk. He had some blankets. Anna brought her food. One day she said, you know why I'm doing this? I love you. I appreciated it, and we had sex...I don't know if I loved her but she saved my life."[47]

Peter F. offers a more detailed retelling of his "first love" in hiding. In September 1944, thirteen year old Peter, a native of Bratislava, went into hiding with a non-Jewish family:

> The family that hid me were working people. The father was a cook. The daughter was of marrying age. I never met them after the war. I probably should have...I read books, mostly, during the day. I was almost thirteen. I thought about girls. Which I didn't have. One day, the daughter of the house brought in a friend of hers, who was about eighteen. And I started to talk to her. I don't know how I managed (I was thirteen, and had no experience) slowly to get her to make love with me. I had no idea how it should be done. It must have been hilarious. If someone watched us, they would have laughed their heads off. Because I didn't know what to do at all. That was happening in 1944/45. When the whole world was in

flames. And as I later learned, none of my family was alive, but I only thought about love-making. Nothing else. [48]

In February 1945, Peter was denounced to the Gestapo by the boyfriend of the family's daughter. Initially deported to a secret camp, he ended up in Theresienstadt. At war's end, he returned to Bratislava, lived with his grandparents, and in 1964, immigrated to Israel, where he became a filmmaker.

Norman S., for his part, posed as a Pole and joined the Polish Army in 1944. He attended an officers' school in Lublin and was assigned to a special unit charged with the liberation of Cracow. His specific task was to discover the location of German mines and then detonate them. One particular set of plans was in the hands of a German woman whom the unit had tracked down. As soon as the information was extracted from this woman, he was instructed to kill her. But, according to his testimony, "this girl was the most beautiful girl I ever saw...I hated her more...I saw my sisters, my girlfriend that they are all dead. Why should this German bitch be alive? This was January 18 [1945]...We started to interrogate her. She wouldn't admit to be German...[referring to one of her interrogators] She said I'm the same as you! I am a Jew!" Norman, however, remained less than convinced, and suggested, in one especially demeaning moment, that she prove that she was circumcised. It was when she began to speak Hebrew and recite the Kol Nidre that he believed her story. The two were married within a year. [49]

Additional commentary from female survivors on relationships in hiding and in resistance groups comes from Ruth P., and Halina B. After Ruth P. escaped Germany and made her way to France, she befriended a French officer and had, in her words, a "little romance, which was a little exciting. We would walk along the beach...very primitive, but very exciting." [50] Halina B. met her husband, Stanislow, while attempting an escape from the Warsaw ghetto in the spring of 1943 (days before the famous uprising). In fact, it was Stanislow, a fighter with the Polish underground, who helped Halina make her way out of the ghetto. Merely by chance did she reconnect with him after the war, stumbling across him in a small Polish fishing town. The two were married in 1946. "He was a brilliant man. The best husband. He wouldn't let me scrub floors...He did that all by himself. He said, 'You went through enough!'" [51]

Sexual Behavior in the Camps

Sexual behavior in the ghettos and hiding places was distinct from such activity in the context of concentration camps, where it was more closely associated with dynamics of power, survival, and abuse. It is therefore debatable whether sexual or romantic relationships in this environment could be viewed as "consensual" in any way. According to Vera Laska, a historian who participated in the anti-Nazi resistance in her native Czechoslovakia during the war, "...The instinct for survival, the primary concern for maintaining one's body alive by supplying it with food, took precedence over any other instinct, including the sexual one...In simpler language, women in concentration camps had one priority; eat to keep alive...This also helps explain the fact that sexual relations were carried on almost exclusively among the camp elite, those who were in a position to 'organize' food at their place of work, in the kitchens, in the Canada detail where the belongings of new arrivals were sorted, or in the field, wherever they cold get their hands directly or indirectly on food..."[52]   The testimony of Irwin U. appears to substantiate these claims. While interned in the Jungfernhof camp in Latvia, he had his first romantic relationship. He insists that this kind of intimacy was pervasive, "provided you were strong enough." "Maybe," in his words, "the relationship helped us through some of the rough spots, but," he cautions, "the primary drive was for food."[53] Irwin maintains contact with his first love, now living in Florida, to this day.

Interestingly, there are numerous testimonies which do not mention the quid pro quo of "sex for food." Interned in the Kielce HASAG labor camp, Sam M., then only a boy, remembers his curiosity over people trying to be intimate in such a difficult setting. "I'm going to say something that I am a little bit embarrassed [by]...I was able to stay in the barracks during the day to sleep...I saw a man and a woman for the first time. We had some women there...I had no idea what they were doing..."[54]   It bears repeating that the severity of the concentration camp environment was a crucial factor in the ability to think of sexual relations, let alone have them. According to Martha V., married couples in the Czech camp, Sered, were allowed to live together, a privilege denied to single women and men, and thus Martha was able to remain with her husband. She "didn't feel alone, even

when [we] were separated."[55]   Interned in the HASAG Apparatenbau of the Pelzery labor camp, Joseph S. took advantage of the little free time he had to meet his wife for clandestine love-making sessions. "People laugh when they see monkeys doing it, but people [are] no different...when you have to do it, you have to do it..."[56]
    Tina B. developed a relationship with a man while interned in the Skarzysko labor camp in 1942.   She remembers seeing him standing all alone one morning: "...[It was] was forty below...Henry was unusual...doesn't have anyone left...He was just wild about his little sister..."[57]   Stella R., too, kindled a romance while in a camp (Novaky in Czechoslovakia).   She recalls arriving at the camp on August 21, but doesn't mention the year, intentionally or not.   The day after her arrival, she spoke to her future husband, Kurt, for the first time.   She met him in the kitchen.   There was, for her, no initial attraction, but they carried on a conversation in German.   "It was a clean-cut courtship...[We both] loved music...and went to Gymnasium...[We] courted in a clean, European way...there is 'Sie' and 'du,' we only used 'Sie.'   I didn't kiss him in the first week." (Stella's interviewer then asks a follow up question about other less formal sexual relationships in the camp that clearly makes Stella uncomfortable, and the subject is quickly dropped, punctuating once again that what is not said during testimony is often as informative as what is said.)[58]   Finally, Ralph Z. recalls a special relationship that developed with a woman named Ruza—while both were imprisoned in Auschwitz.   Ralph apparently received a permit to enter the women's camp as an electrician, but he was prohibited from venturing into any of the areas where there were actual female prisoners.   Defying the ban, Ralph would meet Ruza for a few minutes at a time.   "She was not a girlfriend...We were kissing, but [it] wouldn't go any further...[You] didn't do that in those days."   Ralph saw Ruza after the war, only to find out that she was married and had children.   He told her not to worry.   "That's what happens during war."   Many years later, Ruza made a special effort to visit Ralph, who was living in Montreal.[59]
    On the issue raised by Sybil Milton, that of the myth of liaisons between female prisoners and SS guards, survivor testimony is often unreliable.   When asked by his interviewer about the issue, Georges N., interned in the Wulkow camp, offers only speculation: "The SS did not have sex with Jewish prisoners."   His memory continues with a postwar experience.   "After the war, [I] found out that to get jobs like cleaning the barracks and laundry...some girls...there

was one who danced naked for the camp commandant, so she said. But no touching." Georges also tells the story of the head kapo, who allegedly had a mistress, but it is unclear whether she was a prisoner or came from outside the camp. "She was seen coming out of his barracks. She was a known prostitute. She was on the older side, early thirties."[60] Ella P., maintains that some women had sexual relations with SS officers and that these women were given special privileges, but she has no first hand evidence of this: "There were SS men and women who had relationships. I don't know how far they went, but I'm pretty sure that they did everything they asked for. These women had it easier." Other inmates who were not shown such interest, according to Ella, became resentful while many more simply bristled at the mention of sexual relations with a camp guard.[61] Benny S. likewise heard rumors that an official in the Mielec camp was having an affair with a Jewish prisoner. "I hate to say it, but the head of the camp had an affair with the prettiest women in the barracks. I know one of these women who survived from the barracks. She wasn't more than sixteen years old."[62]

Two eyewitness accounts on this issue come from Irene G. and Danka B. Irene remembers a fellow inmate at Auschwitz by the name of Hinju, whose coerced and illicit relationship with an SS officer saved her life. "Hinju...was as beautiful as Elizabeth Taylor...One day, a train comes in, and she sees her sister with [her] child...Hinju runs to the SS man. The SS man went into the gas chamber and took her sister and her child out. After the war, the SS man wanted to marry her. She didn't want to marry him but she helped him out in a trial [after the war], telling what he did..."[63] Meanwhile, at the Hindenburg camp in Germany, Danka B. implies that soldiers at the camp were interested in her sexually, but that they backed off when they discovered that she was only a teenager. These same guards turned their attention to an older woman, who, according to Danka, was "beautifully built...but...was punished by having to stand in the center of the camp and have her hair shaved as everyone looked on."[64]

In the end, Michael H., incarcerated in Mauthausen, feels that sexual activity in the camp was merely another form of degradation: "One of the men in the Kleiderkammer had access to women. Women and men fell on each other, all the time. Tomorrow we die..." Michael's bunkmates tried to convince him to get a girlfriend, and according to his testimony, he was brought before a line of girls, naked. "One of the girls did go with a man [one of his barracks mates]...They were kept for five hours...naked. The [guy] came back and said he loved the girl he chose." Yet Michael felt sexless and didn't like the process. His friends tried to comfort him by saying, "If we get through this and my wife survives, I'll adopt the girl as my daughter. If not, I'll marry her."[65]

Michael's testimony is an important link to yet another sexual phenomenon in the camps, namely situational homosexuality among prisoners. Vera Laska laments the dearth of survivor commentary particularly about lesbian relationships, but there is abundant discussion of same sex pairings in the testimonies I was able to view. From a linguistic perspective, they suggest the importance of gender analysis once again, as most of the male testimonies (usually heterosexual men who engaged in homosexual activity in the camps) approach their relationships from a perspective of shame, while women, not universally but by and large, appear to be more neutral.

At Mauthausen, Michael H. was a part of a prisoner fire brigade, made up of camp officials and some of the younger, male prisoners. He mentions with great discomfort the fact that the boys in his group would masturbate with each other: "These other bad boys wanted to initiate me into homosexuality...I said...No! No! I'm not going to...I was told by one of these boys that the [guard protecting me]...when he runs out of tickets [to the bordello], he'll want 'you're ass'. The next morning, [they were] evacuating Mauthausen voluntarily." Michal opted to go on the march to avoid what in his eyes was a "fate worse than death.," i.e., homosexuality.[66]

The negative perspective of men in their testimonies towards same sex behavior and attitudes in the camps is the result both of traditional prejudices against homosexuality and the abusive reality of the sexual advances. At Auschwitz, Michael K. was accosted by a Polish Jewish prisoner: "I was from yeshiva. I thought that anyone who would touch my privates was crazy. [This] Polish Jew said, you stupid maggot. You know where your parents are?"[67] Mike W., imprisoned in Ebensee in Austria, served as a kapo—but for only one day, because he was told he needed to "beat up people." He also brushed off the advances of a fellow kapo, a Ukrainian prisoner: "Maybe I was good-looking...[I] gave him a piece of bread. Stupid....He came to me in the nighttime. He proposed me love...[But I] figured out what was going on..."[68] In the Gleiwitz camp, Reinhard F., remembers a kapo who tried to seduce him: "A kapo sent for me...gave me food...asked about my sister...The kapo said he could keep there...suddenly I realized what is up. The kapo said, 'look, I can't take you back now, I'll take you back in the morning...He didn't touch me...'"[69] "Not that pleasant" is how Arthur G. understatedly describes the issue of homosexuality in Blechhammer camp. "I was invited to the second in charge of the camp...[He] limped. Boys would go there at night and would get fed delicacies. One of the boys said, 'would you [Arthur] mind going with us?' I said 'Fine.' I was naïve...This German. He caught wind that everything was not right. Some of the boys were with Germans in another room...I never went back and was never asked to go back."[70]

As mentioned above, accounts of lesbianism are cast in slightly less hostile tones. At Bergen Belsen, according to Phyllis P., there were "a lot of inmates...food was very scarce...there were lesbians carrying on during the night and you could hear it. The situation was so desperate..."[71] From Edith E. at Auschwitz: "I was brought up in a very innocent way. But I learned fast in the camp...[There were] two girls bunking next to me. I couldn't help seeing. It was a new revelation to me. I didn't know such things existed. The inmates took it as it came. They didn't bother. They, the girls were lovely girls."[72] From Fela F. remembers a comparable scene at Auschwitz: "I knew one very smart girl. She was Yugoslav. She was Jewish, and I saw by myself in the nighttime she had a girlfriend, and they made love, and I noticed this..."[73]

Lingering memories of revulsion are not difficult to find, however, among female survivors. Ida T., while in Ravensbrück, had a brief same sex experience with a female prisoner, and the anger in the language of her description is clear. "I was put in a block with political prisoners and lesbians. [There was] absolutely no room...with dysentery and everything...no food, except a green piece of bread and then soup." When Ida arrived at her barrack, one of the prisoners offered to sleep with her in the bunk. She was taken aback, and then horrified, by the ensuing sexual advance. "So...she took me a night before on the bunk. The next day I was out with everybody else...Thank god, she didn't keep me there..."[74]

Conclusion

The volume of survivor testimony and commentary on sexuality and sexual behavior that I was able to survey in the few short years I served as historian at the Shoah Foundation was considerable.

If we gauge the tens of thousands of testimonies awaiting to be catalogued at the Foundation by the yardstick of the few hundred testimonies I viewed, then it safe to assume that an even richer body of narrative and psychological insight will eventually emerge. What is unclear is the extent to which a blanket framework for assessing survivor memories of sexuality assists the work of the historian, linguist, or psychologist. While Langer's model of "common" versus "deep" memory is indeed groundbreaking and indispensable, I believe he overreaches when he argues that the task of making recollections of Holocaust experience coalesce with survivors otherwise "normal" lives is impossible.[75]   Here, the position of LaCapra seems more balanced, even if it is less "uncompromisingly radical or even rigorous" (to use his terms):

> ...the nonfetishistic narrative that resists ideology would involve an active acknowledgement and to some extent an acting out of trauma with the irredeemable losses it brings, and it would indicate its own implication in repetitive processes it cannot entirely transcend. But it would also attempt to conjoin trauma with the possibility of retrieval of desirable aspects of the past that might be of some use in counteracting trauma's extreme effects and in rebuilding individual and social life.[76]

Notes

[1] Lawrence Langer, *Admitting the Holocaust* (New York, 1995), 184.

[2] Dominick LaCapra, *Writing History, Writing Trauma* (Baltimore, 2001), 88, 98, 99.

[3] Sybil Milton, "Women and the Holocaust: The Case of German and German-Jewish Women," in Renate Bridenthal, Atina Grossman, and Marion Kaplan, eds., *When Biology Became Destiny: Women in Weimar and Nazi Germany* (New York, 1984), as reprinted in Carol Rittner and John Roth, *Different Voices: Women and the Holocaust* (St. Paul, Minnesota, 1993), 214-249, 230-231.

[4] Ibid.

[5] Olga Lengyel, "Scientific Experiments," in *Different Voices*, 126

[6] "That sexual activity continued at some level is shown by the ongoing need for contraceptives. A record exists indicating that Jewish ingenuity had found a way to make condoms out of baby pacifiers, the latter being little in demand for their designed use." Charles Roland, *Courage Under Siege: Starvation, Disease, and Death in the Warsaw Ghetto* (New York, 1992), 48.

[7] Dalia Ofer, "Gender Issues in Diaries and Testimonies of the Ghetto: The Case of Warsaw," in Ofer and Lenore Weitzman, *Women in the Holocaust* (New Haven, 1998),163.

[8] Felicja Karay, "Women in the Forced Labor Camps," in Ofer and Weitzman, *Women in the Holocaust*, 297.

[9] Testimony of Tola H., Testimony Number 29381, Survivors of the Shoah Visual History Foundation, Philadelphia, United States, 19 May 1997, 2:12:23-2:15:34, and Testimony of Jack H., Testimony Number, 29378, Survivors of the Shoah Visual History Foundation, Philadelphia, United States, 19 May 1997, 3:13:27-3:16:30. See my article, "Togetherness and Isolation: Holocaust Survivor Memories of Intimacy and Sexuality in the Ghettos," *Oral History Review* 28/1 (Winter/Spring 2001): 1-16.

[10] Testimony of Margarete W., Testimony Number 34418, Survivors of the Shoah Visual History Foundation, New York, United States, 9 October 1997, 02:06:05:16-02:10:54:13.

[11] Testimony of Lennie J., Testimony Number 23717, Survivors of the Shoah Visual History Foundation, Ventura, United States, 2 December 1996, 01:22:39:14-01:26:28:05.

[12] Testimony of David L., Testimony Number, 21550, Survivors of the Shoah Visual History Foundation, Los Angeles, United States, 22 October 1996, 03:17:46:00-03:21:08:00.

[13] Testimony of Irena S., Testimony Number 30898, Survivors of the Shoah Visual History Foundation, San Francisco, United States, 19 July 1997, 02:15:08-02:20:35.

[14] Testimony of Solomon K., Testimony Number 24935, Survivors of the Shoah Visual History Foundation, Mount Vernon, United States, 20 January 1997, 02:17:50-02:20:51.

[15] Testimony of Freda P., Testimony Number 19154, Survivors of the Shoah Visual History Foundation, Calgary, Canada, 27 August 1996, 2:24:44-3:00:10.

[16] Testimony of Emil N., Testimony Number 16680, Survivors of the Shoah Visual History Foundation, Brooklyn, United States, 19 June 1996, 02:18:22-02:22:24; 02:25:13-02:27:46.

[17] Testimony of Rachel D., Testimony Number 18294, Survivors of the Shoah Visual History Foundation, Melbourne, Australia, 5 August 1996, 2:06:05-2:10:03.

[18] Testimony of Sonia F., Testimony Number 23279, Survivors of the Shoah Visual History Foundation, Norfolk, United States, 17 November 1996, 01:22:59:21-01:25:01:15.

[19] Testimony of Cecile K, Testimony Number 23934, Survivors of the Shoah Visual History Foundation, San Rafael, United States, 17 December 1996, 01:17:34:15-01:20:51:04.

[20] The inclusion of the Shanghai ghetto may give readers pause because the conditions here for Jews were better than they were in the ghettos established by the Germans in Poland. However, this difference does not mean that life in the Shanghai district was not a "real" ghetto experience, but rather that it was a unique one within the overall Holocaust narrative.

[21] Testimony of George B., Testimony Number 32487, Survivors of the Shoah Visual History Foundation, Delray Beach, United States, 4 September 1997, 02:17:40-02:21:58.

[22] Testimony of Marc R., Testimony Number 34387, Survivors of the Shoah Visual History Foundation, Scarsdale, United States, 12 October 1997, 3:39:10-3:23:30.

[23] Testimony of Chana W., Testimony Number 18878, Survivors of the Shoah Visual History Foundation, Monticello, United States, 22 August 1996, 2:11:49-2:15:10.

[24] Testimony of Paula P., Testimony Number 30888, Survivors of the Shoah Visual History Foundation, Cote St. Luc, United States, 16 July 1997, 01:23:01:14-01:26:06:06.

[25] Testimony of Irena S.

[26] Testimony of Hanka C., Testimony Number 34766, Survivors of the Shoah Visual History Foundation, Melbourne, Australia, 6 November 1997, 04:11:45:17-04:15:15:02.

[27] Testimony of Jenny C., Testimony Number 3743, Survivors of the Shoah Visual History Foundation, Little Neck, United States, 7 July 1995, 02:20, 03:00-03:17:36. See also "Happy Ending: The Incredible Saga of a Jewish Resistance Fighter in World War II," *New York Magazine* May 17, 1981.

[28] Testimony of Arie T., Testimony Number 22177, Survivors of the Shoah Visual History Foundation, Brooklyn, United States, 6 November 1996, 05:05:52:29-05:07:27:26.

[29] Testimony of Sally S., Testimony Number 23965, Survivors of the Shoah Visual History Foundation, Forrest Hills, United States, 4 December 1996, 02:29:15:28-03:01:48:12.

[30] Testimony of Helen G., Testimony Number 33373, Survivors of the Shoah Visual History Foundation, Caufield, United States, 30 June 1997, 03:23:02:18-03:28:23:14.

[31] Testimony of Rose H., Testimony Number 18630, Survivors of the Shoah Visual History Foundation, Monticello, United States, 16 August 1996, 04:21:21:17-04:24:14:17.

[32] Testimony of Basia W., Testimony Number 22795, Survivors of the Shoah Visual History Foundation, West Hartford, United States, 3 November 1996, 06:00:15:02-06:03:01:01.

[33] Testimony of Mala G., Testimony Number 32613, Survivors of the Shoah Visual History Foundation, Deerfield Beach, United States, 3 September 1997, 05:15:16:18-05:20:52:01.

[34] Testimony of Dresla S., Testimony Number 34416, Survivors of the Shoah Visual History Foundation, New York, United States, 05:00:12:07-05:03:48:11.

[35] Testimony of Mania L., Testimony Number 34002, Survivors of the Shoah Visual History Foundation, Denver, United States, 13 October 1997, 05:11:31:21-05:12:37:18.

[36] Testimony of Minna A., Testimony Number 24637, Survivors of the Shoah Visual History Foundation, Montreal, Canada, 17 December 1996, 05:27:47:20-06:00:04:00.

[37] Testimony of Eva L., Testimony Number 30032, Survivors of the Shoah Visual History Foundation, Melbourne, Australia, 4 April 1997, 03:27:06:28-04:02:27:12.

[38] Interview with Sol R., Testimony Number 10098, Survivors of the Shoah Visual History Foundation, Monroe, United States, 9 March 1996, 02:18:00-02:25:00.

[39] Ibid., 03:09:16-03:14:38.

[40] Norbert Troller, *Theresienstadt: Hitler's Gift to the Jews* (North Carolina, 1991), 90.

[41] Interview with Kurt T., Testimony Number 28104, Survivors of the Shoah Visual History Foundation, Boca Raton, United States, 15 April 1997, 04:12:45-04:14:59.

[42] Interview with Dina G., Testimony Number 46122, Survivors of the Shoah Visual History Foundation, Felton, United States, 26 September 1998, 04:24:21-04:27:08.

[43] Ibid. , 07:27:14:19-08:02:08:06

[44] Ibid. , 08:07:52:27-08:10:02:09

[45] Testimony of Ernest S., Testimony Number 23340, Survivors of the Shoah Visual History Foundation, Westport, United States, 11 December 1996, 01:28:29:29-02:04:34:10.

[46] Testimony of Mark N., Testimony Number 21334, Survivors of the Shoah Visual History Foundation, Hallandale, United States, 13 October 1996, 03:19:32:18-03:23:23:24.

[47] Testimony of Frank S., Testimony Number 21382, Survivors of the Shoah Visual History Foundation, Hackensack, United States, 14 October 1996, 03:21:26:13-03:23:49:14.

[48] Testimony of Peter F., Testimony Number 29384, Survivors of the Shoah Visual History Foundation, Tel Aviv, Israel, 12 June 1997, 02:04:43:17-02:08:02:17.

[49] Testimony of Norman S., Testimony Number 03331, Survivors of the Shoah Visual History Foundation, Springfield, United States, 9 June 1995.

[50] Testimony of Ruth P., Testimony Number 19973, Survivors of the Shoah Visual History Foundation, 7 September 1996, San Clemente, United States, 03:09:15:05-03:15:41:07.

[51] Testimony of Halina B., Testimony Number 31545, Survivors of the Shoah Visual History Foundation, Brooklyn, United States, 31 July 1997, 04:10:28:25-04:16:34:17.

[52] Vera Laska, "Women 264

[53] Testimony of Irwin U., Testimony Number 3959, Survivors of the Shoah Visual History Foundation, 02:13:53:09-02:16:35:20.

[54] Testimony of Sam M., Testimony Number 29441, Survivors of the Shoah Visual History Foundation, Brooklyn, United States, 2 June 1997, 02:19:52:17-02:24:59:28.

[55] Testimony of Martha V., Testimony Number 33145, Survivors of the Shoah Visual History Foundation, Toronto, Canada, 20 August 1997, 03:19:27:28-03:23:04:1.

[56] Testimony of Joseph S., Testimony Number 29094, Survivors of the Shoah Visual History Foundation, New Orleans, United States, 20 May 1997, 03:09:32;13-03:11:16:13.

[57] Testimony of Tina B., Testimony Number 18766, Survivors of the Shoah Visual History Foundation, Monticello, United States, 21 August 1996, 02:24:16:12-02:29:30:10.

[58] Testimony of Stella R., Testimony Number 33804, Survivors of the Shoah Visual History Foundation, Baltimore, United States, 14 September 1997, 04:29:19:06-05:05:11:18.

[59] Testimony of Ralph Z., Testimony Number 22735, Survivors of the Shoah Visual History Foundation, Hampstead, United States, 14 November 1996, 05:11:48:05-05:15:01:19.

[60] Testimony of Georges N., Testimony Number 40908, Survivors of the Shoah Visual History Foundation, 08:27:06:22-09:02:07:08.

[61] Testimony of Ella P., Testimony Number 30825, Survivors of the Shoah Visual History Foundation, Philadelphia, United States, 16 July 1997, 03:04:52:03-03:08:27:05.
[62] Testimony of Benny S., Testimony Number 18403, Survivors of the Shoah Visual History Foundation, Monticello, United States, 12 August 1996, 02:16:13:19-02:19:05:20.
[63] Testimony of Irene G., Testimony Number 27951, Survivors of the Shoah Visual History Foundation , Rosslyn, United States, 6 April 1997, 03:23:06:16-03:25:17:29.
[64] Testimony of Danka B., Testimony Number 32115, Survivors of the Shoah Visual History Foundation, Aberdeen, Scotland, 7 June 1997, 03:14:59:02-03:20:43:22.
[65] Testimony of Michael H., Testimony Number 26562, Survivors of the Shoah Visual History Foundation, Amersham, United States, 23 January 1997, 13:16:03:17-13:21:17:27
[66] Ibid. 10:21:53-10:25
[67] Testimony of Michael K., Testimony Number 23286, Survivors of the Shoah Visual History Foundation, Brookline, United States, 21 November 1996, 03:17:29:10-03:21:22:15.
[68] Testimony of Mike W., Testimony Number 26, Survivors of the Shoah Visual History Foundation, Van Nuys, United States, 22 July 1994, 02:07:58:15-02:12:19:03.
[69] Testimony of Reinhard F., Testimony Number 28165, Survivors of the Shoah Visual History Foundation, Cambridge, United States, 24 April 1997, 03:08:27:07-03:11:21:26.
[70] Testimony of Arthur G., Testimony Number 24368, Survivors of the Shoah Visual History Foundation, Pepper Pike, United States, 17 December 1996, 03:26:08:13-03:29:35:05.
[71] Testimony of Phyllis P., Testimony Number 24202, Survivors of the Shoah Visual History Foundation, Delray Beach, United States, 16 December 1996, 02:19:13:09-2:23:38:05.
[72] Testimony of Edith E., Testimony Number 31209, Survivors of the Shoah Visual History Foundation, Baltimore, United States, 16 July 1997, 03:10:03:22-03:13:22:06.
[73] Testimony of Fela F., Testimony Number 39604, Survivors of the Shoah Visual History Foundation, Melbourne, Australia, 3 March 1998, 04:03:57:28-04:07:33:28.
[74] Testimony of Ida T., Testimony Number 7712, Survivors of the Shoah Visual History Foundation, 04:18:46:15-04:21:48:28.
[75] Lawrence Langer, *Holocaust Testimonies: The Ruins of Memory* (New Haven, 1991), 2, 3.

[76] Dominick LaCapra, *Representing the Holocaust: History, Theory, Trauma* (Cornell, 1994), 199, LaCapra, *Writing History, Writing Trauma* (Baltimore, 2001), 88, 98, 99, and Langer, *Admitting the Holocaust* (New York, 1995), 184.

Conclusion

Questions of truthfulness lie at the heart of oral history's problem as a source. While survivors bring a level of believability to a story when they say that something happened directly to them or when they can situate an event in a specific time and place, there is never a guarantee that their story is accurate or true. Even the often-used gauges of consistency and likelihood have little meaning in the context of the Holocaust, in the absence spatial and temporal constants, and where the ineffable and the undoable were possible. Despite this very real problem of verification, however, non-Holocaust-connected studies on the effect of trauma and positive and negative stresses on the human psyche reveal that memories of cataclysmic events tend to be more accurate than those of ordinary ones, at least in a broad sense. According to Harvard psychologist, Daniel Schacter, when a person experiences trauma, the essence of it is almost always well-remembered, and if there is any distortion, it is most frequently in specific details. This unusually accurate recall, Schacter claims, can be traced to the release of stress-related hormones, singled by the brain's "emotional computer," the amygdala.[1] It would seem, then, that events impacting such a central pillar of our existence as sexuality would elicit rather precise recollections (unless of course we proceed from the assumption that all survivors are incapable of telling the truth or intentionally trying to mislead, in which case the threshold of believability, indeed all epistemological value, would be raised to a level far beyond that imparted to written documents).

More importantly, as I argued at the beginning of this collection, the choice of words and the emotions exhibited when a survivor speaks of an event are as significant from an analytical perspective as the content of the narrative. Oren Baruch Stier reminds us that survivor memory is often "converted into speech (and gesture, and silence, and a host of subtle visual cues) for the first time, and it is thus profoundly self-reflexive. This may often involve a process of self-translation; events experienced and processed in European languages are now expressed in the vernacular, usually English for the majority of the current archiving projects. Thus, we watch as the testimony unfolds into a narrative, we see how the survivor struggles to find the right language to express her memory."[2] Psychologist Henry Greenspan makes a similar point:

> ...[There is an] unmistakable quality of personal ownership that characterizes their retelling...It is as though the recounter were saying, 'This is *my* story,' salvaged in memory for some particular reasons and later retold in order to make some particularly vital point.[3]

On a most basic level, the, Holocaust testimony tells us a great deal about how we as humans build and rebuild the past amidst our own linguistic limitations.

What can no longer be claimed is that survivor memory adds little or nothing to the Holocaust narrative or may simply be distracting for today's researchers. For the purposes of this collection of essays, it is clear that sexuality and other issues affecting women as women and men as men were facets of everyday life during the Nazi terror, and that memories of sexuality and related themes are occasionally the central nexus points between survival and death. For some, sexuality was *the* road to survival. For others, it lay at the core of their dehumanization. And still for others, sexuality stood for the possibility of all that was supposed to be good about life and all that was ultimately taken away.

Notes

[1] Daniel Schacter, *Searching for Memory: The Brain, the Mind, and the Past* (New York, 1996), 205, 209, 216.
[2] Oren Baruch Stier, "Framing the Witness: The Memorial Role of Holocaust Video Testimonies," in John Roth and Elisabeth Maxwell, eds., *Remembering for the Future: The Holocaust in an Age of Genocide* (New York, 2001), 192.
[3] Henry Greenspan, *On Listening to Holocaust Survivors* (Westport, Conn., 1998), 12, 13.

Select Bibliography

Primary Sources

Survivors of the Shoah Visual History Foundation Testimonies (a selection):

Abraham B., Testimony Number 18061
Alex C., Testimony Number 20021
Arie T., Testimony Number 22177
Arthur G., Testimony Number 24368
Basia W., Testimony Number 22795
Bebe F., Testimony Number 33191
Benesch T., Testimony Number 25895
Benny S., Testimony Number 18403
Bernard Z., Testimony Number 35123
Bianka K., Testimony Number 13723
Bina W., Testimony Number 33960
Bronia S., Testimony Number 10747
Bronka K., Testimony Number 29421
Cecile K, Testimony Number 23934
Chana W., Testimony Number 18878
Chasia K., Testimony Number 34767
Clare G., Testimony Number 24434
Coenraad R., Testimony Number 18548
Dana S., Testimony Number 14894
Danka B., Testimony Number 32115
David L., Testimony Number, 21550
Deborah S., Testimony Number 25384

Dina G., Testimony Number 46122
Doba A., Testimony Number 29753
Douglas F., Testimony Number 29788
Dresla S., Testimony Number 34416
Edith E., Testimony Number 31209
Ella P., Testimony Number 30825
Emil N., Testimony Number 16680
Erika G., Testimony Number 25797
Ernst S., Testimony Number 23340,
Eugene L., Testimony Number 28052
Eva L., Testimony Number 30032
Eva S., Testimony Number 21666,
Eva S., Testimony Number 23853
Eva S., Testimony Number 33024
Fanny L., Testimony Number 42751
Fela F., Testimony Number 39604
Fela P., Testimony Number 33606
Frank S., Testimony Number 21382
Freda P., Testimony Number 19154
Gad B.
George B., Testimony Number 32487
Georges N., Testimony Number 40908
Germaine P., Testimony Number 33265,
Gerri M., Testimony Number 6518
Gina L., Testimony Number 31586
Golda N., Testimony Number 30054
Greta K., Testimony Number 26524
Halina B., Testimony Number 31545
Hanka C., Testimony Number 34766
Hans-Oskar L., PCN Number 23442,
Harry B., Testimony Number 33336
Helen G., Testimony Number 33373
Helene U., Testimony Number 20200
Helene U., Testimony Number 20200
Hermann S., Testimony Number 14480
Herta M., Testimony Number 18043
Huguette F. Testimony Number 24766
Ibolya S.
Ida T., Testimony Number 7712
Ilse A.

Imre H., Testimony Number 8500
Inge F., Testimony Number 11083
Irena S., Testimony Number 30898
Irene G., Testimony Number 27951
Irmgard K.
Irwin U., Testimony Number 3959
Israel W., Testimony Number 26908
Jack H., Testimony Number 29378
Jack O., Testimony Number 20926
Janos S., Testimony Number 18090
Jean S., Testimony Number 32842,
Jenny C., Testimony Number 3743
Joan W., Testimony Number 20213
Johann H., PCN Number 632747
Joseph S., Testimony Number 29094
Judith B., Testimony Number 31699
Klara N., PCN Number 627760
Kurt K., Testimony Number 26097
Kurt T., Testimony Number 28104
Lennie J., Testimony Number 23717
Linda M., Testimony Number 17987
Luba L., Testimony Number 34921
Luba S., Testimony Number 18672
Magda S., Testimony Number 18057,
Magdalena V., Testimony Number 18311
Mala G., Testimony Number 32613
Malka W., Testimony Number 42723
Mania L., Testimony Number 34002
Marc R., Testimony Number 34387
Margarete W., Testimony Number 34418
Marie P., Testimony Number 33263
Mark N., Testimony Number 21334
Martha V., Testimony Number 33145
Mary W, Testimony Number 8123
Michael H., Testimony Number 26562
Michael K., Testimony Number 23286
Mike W., Testimony Number 26
Mina L., Testimony Number 18757
Minna A., Testimony Number 24637
Nathan O., Testimony Number 20084

Nellie A., Testimony Number 30733
Norman S., Testimony Number 03331
Paula H., Testimony Number 33422
Paula P., Testimony Number 30888
Peter F., Testimony Number 29384
Peter S.
Phyllis L., Testimony Number 31585
Phyllis P., Testimony Number 24202
Rachel D., Testimony Number 18294
Rachela P., Testimony Number 27003
Ralph Z., Testimony Number 22735
Reinhard F., Testimony Number 28165
Rena G., Testimony Number 19221
Rita H., Testimony Number 30717
Rose H., Testimony Number 18630
Ruth P., Testimony Number 19973
Sabina M., Testimony Number 17323
Sally S., Testimony Number 23965
Sam M., Testimony Number 29441
Sara W., Testimony Number 19447
Sarah W., Testimony Number 27204
Shary N., Testimony Number 21203
Sigmund T., Testimony Number 35109
Sol R., Testimony Number 10098
Solomon K., Testimony Number 24935
Sonia F., Testimony Number 23279
Stefan K., PCN 25053,
Stella R., Testimony Number 33804
Tina B., Testimony Number 18766
Toby K., Testimony Number 30719,
Tola H., Testimony Number 29381
Walter G., Testimony Number 33330
William D., Testimony Number 32569

Secondary Sources

Ballinger, Pamela. "The Culture of Survivors: Post-Traumatic Stress Disorder and Traumatic Memory," *History and Memory* 10/2 (1998): 99-132.

Bettelheim, Bruno. *The Informed Heart: Autonomy in a Mass Age.* New York, 1960.

Bridenthal, Renate, Atina Grossman, and Marion Kaplan, eds. *When Biology Became Destiny: Women in Weimar and Nazi Germany.* New York, 1984.

Burleigh, Michael, ed. *Confronting the Nazi Past: New Debates on Modern German History.* London, 1996.

Burleigh, Michael. "Eugenic Utopias and the Genetic Present," *Totalitarian Movements and Political Religions* 1/1 (Summer 2000): 69.

Büttner, Ursula. *Die Not der Juden teilen: Christlich-jüdische Familien im Dritten Reich.* Hamburg, 1988.

Diner, Dan. "Memory and Method: Variance in Holocaust Narrations," *Studies in Contemporary Jewry* 13 (1997): 84-99.

Foucault, Michel. *Power/Knowledge : Selected Interviews and Other Writings, 1972-1977.* New York, 1980.

Frankl, Viktor. *Man's Search for Meaning.* New York, 1952.

Friedländer, Saul. "The Shoah Between Memory and History," *Jerusalem Quarterly* 53 (1990): 115-126.

-----. "Trauma, Transference, and 'Working Through' in Writing the History of the Shoah," *History and Memory* 4/1 (Spring/Summer 1992): 55.

Friedman, Jonathan. "Togetherness and Isolation: Holocaust Survivor Memories of Intimacy and Sexuality in the Ghettos," *Oral History Review* 28/1 (Winter/Spring 2001): 1-16.

Gilman, Sander. *The Jew's Body.* New York, 1991.

Goodhart, Sandor. "The Witness of Trauma: A Review Essay," *Modern Judaism* 12/2 (1992): 203-217.

Greenspan, Henry. *On Listening to Holocaust Survivors.* Westport, Conn., 1998.

Grossman, Atina, "Trauma, Memory, and Motherhood: Germans and Jewish Displaced Persons in Post Nazi Germany, 1945-

1949," *Archiv für Sozialgeschichte* 38 (1998): 215-241.

Hartman, Geoffrey. "About the 'Survivors of the Shoah Visual History Foundation,'" *Cahier International* (December 1998): 82-85.

Heinemann, Marlene. *Gender and Destiny: Women Writers and the Holocaust.* Westport, Conn., 1986.

Heger, Heinz. *The Men with the Pink Triangle.* London, 1980.

Johansson, Warren and William Percy, "Homosexuals in Nazi Germany," *Simon Wiesenthal Center Annual* 7 (1990): 225-63.

Kaplan, Marion. *Between Dignity and Despair: Jewish Life in Nazi Germany.* Oxford, 1998.

Koch, Gertrud. "'Against All Odds' or the Will to Survive," *History and Memory* 9/1 and 2 (1997): 393-408.

LaCapra, Dominick. *History and Memory After Auschwitz.* Ithaca, 1998.

-----. *Representing the Holocaust: History, Theory, Trauma.* Cornell, 1994.

-----. *Writing History, Writing Trauma.* Baltimore, 2001.

Langer, Lawrence. *Admitting the Holocaust.* New York, 1995.

-----. *Holocaust Testimonies: The Ruins of Memory.* New Haven, 1991.

Maiwald, Stefan and Gerd Mischler, *Sexualität unter dem Hakenkreuz: Manipulation und Vernichtung der Intimsphäre im NS-Staat.* Hamburg, 1999.

Ofer, Dalia and Lenore Weitzman, eds. *Women in the Holocaust.* New Haven, 1998.

Rainer Pommerin, *Sterilisierung der Rheinlandbastarde: Das Schicksal einer farbigen deutschen Minderheit, 1918-1937.* Düsseldorf, 1979.

Des Pres, Terence. *The Survivor.* New York, 1976.

Proctor, Robert. *Racial Hygiene: Medicine under the Nazis.* Cambridge, Mass., 1988.

Rethmeier, Andreas. *Nürnberger Rassengesetze und Entrechtung der Juden im Zivilrecht.* Frankfurt, 1995.

Ringelheim, Joan. "The Holocaust: Taking Women into Account," *Jewish Quarterly* (Autumn 1992): 19-23

Rittner, Carol and John Roth, eds. *Different Voices: Women and the Holocaust.* St. Paul, Minnesota, 1993.

Roland, Charles. *Courage Under Siege: Starvation, Disease, and*

Death in the Warsaw Ghetto. New York, 1992.

Schacter, Daniel. *Searching for Memory: The Brain, the Mind, and the Past.* New York, 1996.

Schwertfeger, Ruth. *Women of Theresienstadt: Voices from a Concentration Camp.* New York, 1989.

Shapira, Anita. "The Holocaust: Private Memories, Public Memory," *Jewish Social Studies* 4/2 (1998): 40-58.

Stier, Oren Baruch. "Framing the Witness: The Memorial Role of Holocaust Video Testimonies," in John Roth and Elisabeth Maxwell, eds. *Remembering for the Future: The Holocaust in an Age of Genocide.* New York, 2001.

Stolzfus, Nathan. *Resistance of the Heart: Intermarriage and the Rosenstrasse Protest in Nazi Germany.* New York, 1996.

Tonkin, Elizabeth. *Narrating Our Pasts: The Social Construction of Oral History.* Cambridge, 1992.

Troller, Norbert. *Theresienstadt: Hitler's Gift to the Jews.* North Carolina, 1991.

Weindling, Paul. *Health, Race, and German Politics Between National Unification and Nazism.* Cambridge, 1989.

White, Hayden. *The Content of the Form: Narrative Discourse and Historical Representation.* Baltimore, 1987.

Index